Best
Garden Plants
for
Michigan

Tim Wood & Alison Beck

LONE
PINE

Lone Pine Publishing International

© 2005 by Lone Pine Publishing International Inc.
First printed in 2005   10 9 8 7 6 5 4 3 2 1
Printed in Canada

The Distributor: Lone Pine Publishing
1808 B Street NW, Suite 140
Auburn, WA, USA 98001

Website: www.lonepinepublishing.com

Library and Archives Canada Cataloguing in Publication
Wood, Tim (Timothy D.), 1960-
    Best garden plants for Michigan / Tim Wood, Alison Beck.

Includes index.
ISBN-13: 978-1-55105-498-8.--
ISBN-10: 1-55105-498-1

. 1. Plants, Ornamental--Michigan. 2. Gardening--Michigan.
I. Beck, Alison, 1971- II. Title.

SB453.2.M5W66 2005   635.9'09774   C2005-902073-3

Scanning & Electronic Film: Elite Lithographers Co.

Photography: all photos by **Tim Matheson** and **Tamara Eder** except **AASelection** 31a; **Bailey Nursery Roses** 120a; **Sandra Bit** 145a; **Conard-Pyle Roses** 120b, 124a&b; **Joan de Grey** 45a, 52b; **Don Doucette** 113b; **EuroAmerican** 33a; **Derek Fell** 30a, 61a&b, 165a&b; **Jen Fafard** 144a; **Erika Flatt** 58, 95a, 139a, 140b, 166b; **Anne Gordon** 163a; **Horticolor** 52a; **Duncan Kelbaugh** 140a; **Liz Klose** 148a, 149a&b, 158a, 159a, 170a; **Dawn Loewen** 66a, 77a, 81a, 84a&b, 175a; **Marilynn McAra** 144b; **Kim O'Leary** 22a, 24a&b, 142a, 151b; **Allison Penko** 54a, 72b, 77b, 88a, 94b, 96b, 107a&b, 112b, 130b, 138b, 139b, 143a, 160a&b, 161a&b, 162a, 164b, 167a; **Laura Peters** 42a, 67a&b, 78a, 79a, 92b, 96a, 131a&b, 134a, 145b, 147a&b, 148b, 150a&b, 152a&b, 153a&b, 154a&b, 156, 158b, 159b, 162b, 163b, 164a, 166a, 167b, 168a&b, 170b, 174c, 175c; **Robert Ritchie** 48a&b, 68b, 70a, 87a&b, 102a, 117a&b, 126a, 151a; **Leila Sidi** 28a&b, 146b; **Peter Thompstone** 18a, 26a, 49a, 63b; **Mark Turner** 69b; **Tim Wood** 8b, 68a, 69a, 70b, 75a, 85a, 104a&b, 105a, 109a, 110a, 114a&b, 135a&b, 136a; **Don Williamson** 134b, 141a&b.

Front Cover Photographs (clockwise from top left): Erika Flatt, lily; Tamara Eder, rose, bearded iris, daylily; Allison Penko, daylily; Laura Peters, lily; Tim Matheson, dahlia

Front Cover Background Photographs: Tim Matheson, crabapple (top); Tamara Eder, lilac (middle), sweet potato vine (bottom)

PC: P1

Table of Contents

Introduction

Starting a garden can seem like a daunting task, but it's also an exciting and rewarding adventure. With so many plants to choose from, the challenge is to decide which ones and how many you can include in your garden. This book is intended to give beginning gardeners the information they need to start planning and planting gardens of their own. It includes a wide variety of plants and provides basic plant descriptions, planting and growing information and tips for use. With this book in hand, you can begin to produce a beautiful and functional landscape in your own yard.

Michigan has a temperate climate; the summer growing season is long and warm, and cold winters ensure a good period of dormancy and plenty of flowers in spring. Rainfall is fairly predictable, and the soil, though not without its challenges, supports a variety of plants.

Hardiness zones and frost dates are two terms often used when discussing climate and gardening. Hardiness zones are based on the minimum possible winter temperatures. Plants are rated based on the zones in which they grow successfully. The last frost date in spring combined with the first frost date in fall allows us to predict the length of the growing season and gives us an idea of when we can begin planting.

Microclimates are small areas that are generally warmer or colder than the surrounding area. Buildings, fences, trees and other large structures can provide extra shelter in winter but may trap heat in summer, thus creating a warmer microclimate. The bottoms of hills are usually colder than the tops but may not be as windy. Take advantage of these areas when you plan your garden and choose your plants; you may even grow out-of-zone plants successfully in a warm, sheltered location.

Getting Started

When planning your garden, start with a quick analysis of the garden as it is now. Plants have different requirements and it is best to put the right plant in the right place rather than to try to change your garden to suit the plants you want.

Knowing which parts of your garden receive the most and least amounts of sunlight will help you to choose the proper plants and to decide where to plant them. Light is classified into four basic groups: full sun (direct, unobstructed light all or most of the day); partial shade (direct sun for about half the day and shade for the rest); light shade (shade all or most of the day with some sun filtering through to ground level); and full shade (no direct sunlight). Most plants prefer a certain amount of light, but many can adapt to a range of light levels.

The soil is the foundation of a good garden. Plants use the soil to hold

themselves upright but also rely on the many resources it contains: air, water, nutrients, organic matter and a host of microbes. The soil particle size influences the amount of air, water and nutrients the soil can hold. Sand, with the largest particles, has a lot of air space and allows water and nutrients to drain quickly. Clay, with the smallest particles, is high in nutrients but has very little air space. Water is therefore slow to penetrate clay and slow to drain from it.

Soil acidity or alkalinity (measured on the pH scale) influences the amount and type of nutrients available to plants. A pH of 7 is neutral; a lower pH is more acidic. Most plants prefer a soil with a pH of 5.5–7.5. Soil-testing

USDA Hardiness Zones Map

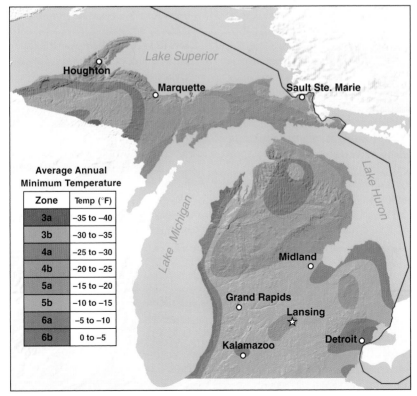

Average Annual Minimum Temperature

Zone	Temp (°F)
3a	−35 to −40
3b	−30 to −35
4a	−25 to −30
4b	−20 to −25
5a	−15 to −20
5b	−10 to −15
6a	−5 to −10
6b	0 to −5

kits are available at most garden centers, and soil samples can be sent to testing facilities for a more thorough analysis. This will give you an idea of what plants will do well in your soil and what amendments your soil might need.

Compost is one of the best and most important amendments you can add to any type of soil. Compost improves soil by adding organic matter and nutrients, introducing soil microbes, increasing water retention and improving drainage. You can purchase compost or you can make it in your own backyard.

Selecting Plants

It's important to purchase healthy plants that are free of pests and diseases. Such plants will establish quickly in your garden and will not introduce problems that may spread to other plants. You should have a good idea of what the plant is supposed to look like—the color and shape of the leaves and the habit of the plant—and then inspect the plant for signs of disease or insect damage before buying it.

The majority of plants are container grown. This is an efficient way for nurseries and greenhouses to grow plants, but when plants grow in a restricted space for too long, they can become pot bound with their roots densely encircling the inside of the pot. Avoid purchasing plants in this condition; they are often stressed and can take longer to establish. It is often possible to temporarily remove the pot to look at the condition of the plant roots. You can check for soil-borne insects, rotten roots and girdling or pot-bound roots at the same time. Roots that are wrapped densely around the inside of a pot must be lightly pruned or teased apart before planting.

Planting Basics

The following tips apply to all plants.
• Prepare the garden before planting. Remove weeds, make any needed amendments and dig or till the soil in preparation for planting if you are starting a new landscape. This may be more difficult in established beds to which you want to add a single plant. The prepared area should be the size of the plant's mature root system.
• Settle the soil with water. Good contact between the roots and the soil is important, but if you press the soil down too firmly, as often happens when you step on the soil, you can cause compaction, which reduces the movement of water through the soil and leaves very few air spaces. Instead, pour water in as you fill the hole with soil. The water will settle the soil evenly without allowing it to compact.
• Unwrap the roots. It is always best to remove any container before

1. Gently remove container.

2. Ensure proper planting depth.

3. Backfill with soil.

planting to give the roots a chance to spread out naturally when planted. In particular, you should remove plastic containers, fiber pots, wire and burlap before planting trees. Fiber pots decompose very slowly, if at all, and they wick moisture away from the plant. Burlap may be synthetic, which won't decompose, and wire can eventually strangle the roots as they mature. The only exceptions to this rule are the peat pots and pellets used to start annuals and vegetables; these decompose and can be planted with the young transplants. Even these peat pots should be sliced down the sides and any part of the pot that will be exposed above ground should be removed to prevent water from being wicked away from the roots.

- Accommodate the rootball. If you prepared your planting area ahead of time so it will accommodate the mature roots, your planting hole will only need to be big enough to accommodate the rootball with the roots spread out slightly.
- Know the mature size of your plants. You should space your plants based on how big the plants will be when they are mature rather than how big they are when you plant them. The accounts mention the mature size of plants; this is the amount of space you will need to give the plant, not just enough space for its immature size at planting. For example, a shrub that will grow to be 10' tall and wide may only be 12" when you buy and plant it. Large plants should have enough room to mature without interfering with walls, roof overhangs, power lines, walkways and surrounding plants.
- Plant at the same depth. Plants generally like to grow at a certain level in relation to the soil and should be planted at the same level they were at in the pot or container before you transplanted them.
- Identify your plants. Keep track of what's what in your garden by putting a tag next to each plant when you plant it. A gardening journal is also a great place to list the plants you have and where you planted them. It is very easy, for beginning and seasoned gardeners alike, to forget exactly what they planted and where they planted it.
- Water deeply. It's better to water deeply once every week or two, depending on the plant, than to water a bit more often. Deep and thorough watering forces roots to grow as they search for water and helps them survive dry spells when water bans may restrict your watering regime. Always check the rootzone before you water as some soils hold more water for longer periods than

4. Settle backfilled soil with water.

5. Water the plant well.

6. Add a layer of mulch.

other soils. More gardeners overwater than underwater. Mulching helps retain moisture and reduces watering needs. Containers are the watering exception as they can quickly dry out and may even need watering every day.

Michigan herb garden

Choosing Plants

When choosing your plants, try to aim for a variety of sizes, shapes, textures, features and bloom times. Features, such as decorative fruit, variegated or colorful leaves and interesting bark, provide interest when plants aren't blooming. This way you will have a garden that captivates your attention all year.

False cypress

Annuals

Annuals are planted new each year and are only expected to last for a single growing season. Their flowers and decorative foliage provide bright splashes of color and can fill in spaces around immature trees, shrubs and perennials.

Annuals are easy to plant and are usually sold in small cell-packs of four or six plants. The roots quickly fill the space in these small packs, so the small rootball should be broken up before planting. Split the ball in two up the center or run your thumb up each side to break up the roots.

Many annuals are grown from seed and can be started directly in the garden once the soil has begun to warm up.

Perennials

Perennials grow for three or more years. They usually die back to the ground each fall and send up new shoots in spring, though they can also be evergreen or semi-shrubby. They often have a shorter period of bloom than annuals but require less care.

Many perennials benefit from being divided every few years, usually in early spring while plants are still dormant or, with some plants, after flowering. This keeps them growing and blooming vigorously, and in some cases controls their spread. Dividing involves digging the plant up, removing dead debris, breaking the plant into several pieces using a sharp knife, spade or saw and replanting some or all of the pieces. Extra pieces can be shared with family, friends and neighbors. Consult a perennial book, such as *Perennials for Michigan*, for further information on the care of perennials.

Trees & Shrubs

Trees and shrubs provide the bones of the garden. They are often the slowest growing plants but usually live the longest. Characterized by leaf type, they may be deciduous or evergreen, and needled or broad-leaved.

Trees should have as little disturbed soil as possible at the bottom of the planting hole. Loose dirt settles over time and sinking even an inch can kill some trees. The prepared area for trees and shrubs needs to be at least two to four times bigger than the rootball.

Staking, sometimes recommended for newly planted trees, is only necessary for trees over 5' tall. Stakes support the rootball until it grows enough to support the tree. Stakes should allow the trunk to move with the wind.

Pruning is more often required for shrubs than trees. It helps them maintain an attractive shape and can improve blooming. Consult a book, such as *Tree and Shrub Gardening for Michigan*, for information about pruning trees and shrubs.

Roses

Roses are beautiful shrubs with lovely, often fragrant blooms. Traditionally, most roses only bloomed once in the growing season but new varieties bloom all, or almost all, summer. Repeat-blooming, or recurrent, roses should be deadheaded to encourage more flower production. One-time bloomers should be left for the colorful hips that develop.

Generally, roses prefer a fertile, well-prepared planting area. A rule of thumb is to prepare an area 24" across, front to back and side to side, and 24" deep. Add plenty of compost or other fertile organic matter and keep roses well watered during the growing season. Many roses are quite durable and will adapt to poorer conditions. Grafted roses should be planted with the graft two inches below the soil line. When watering, avoid getting

a well-maintained Michigan garden

water on the foliage to reduce the spread of blackspot.

Roses, like all shrubs, have specific pruning requirements. Consult a book, such as *Roses for Michigan*, for detailed information.

Vines

Vines or climbing plants are useful for screening and shade, especially in a location too small for a tree. They may be woody or herbaceous and annual or perennial. Vines may cling to surfaces, may have wrapping tendrils or stems, or may need to be tied in place with string.

Sturdy trellises, arbors, porch railings, fences, walls, poles and trees are all possible vine supports. If a support is needed, ensure it's in place before you plant the vine to avoid disturbing the roots later. Choose a support that is suitable for the vine you are growing. The support needs to be sturdy enough to hold the plant up and should match the growing habit of the vine—whether clinging, wrapping or tied.

Bulbs, Corms & Tubers

These plants have fleshy, underground storage organs that allow them to survive extended periods of dormancy. They are often grown for the bright splashes of color their flowers provide. They may be spring, summer or fall flowering. Each has an ideal depth and time of year at which it should be planted.

Hardy bulbs can be left in the ground and will flower every year. Some popular, tender plants are grown from bulbs, corms or tubers and are generally lifted from the garden in late summer or fall as the foliage dies back. These are stored in a cool, frost-free location for winter, to be replanted in spring.

Herbs

Herbs are plants with medicinal, culinary or other economic purposes. A few common culinary herbs are included in this book. Even if you don't cook with herbs, the often-fragrant foliage adds its aroma to the

a colorful foundation garden

garden, and the plants can be quite decorative in form, leaf and flower. A conveniently placed container of your favorite herbs—perhaps located near the kitchen door—will yield plenty of flavor and fragrance all summer.

Many herbs have pollen-producing flowers that attract butterflies, bees, hummingbirds and predatory insects to your garden. Predatory insects feast on problem insects, such as aphids, mealybugs and whiteflies.

Foliage Plants

Many plants are grown for their decorative foliage rather than their flowers, which may also be decorative. Ornamental grasses, ferns, groundcovers and other foliage plants add a variety of colors, textures and forms to the garden. Many of these are included in other sections of this book, but we have set aside a few for the unique touch their foliage adds to the garden.

Ornamental grasses and grass-like plants provide interest all year when the withered blades are left to stand all winter. They are cut back in early spring and divided when the clumps begin to die out in the centers.

Ferns provide a lacy foliage accent and combine attractively with broad-leaved perennials and shrubs. Ferns are a common sight in moist and shady gardens, but some varieties will survive in full sun.

A Final Comment

The more you discover about the fascinating world of plants—whether from reading books, talking to other gardeners, appreciating the creative designs of others, or experimenting with something new in your own garden—the more rewarding your gardening experience will become. This book is intended as a guide to germinate and grow your passion for plants.

Angelonia
Angelonia

'Alba' (above), 'Blue Pacific' (below)

With its loose, airy spikes of orchid-like flowers, angelonia makes a welcome addition to the garden.

Growing

Angelonia prefers **full sun** but tolerates a bit of shade. The soil should be **fertile, moist** and **well drained**. Although this plant grows naturally in damp areas, such as along ditches and near ponds, it is fairly drought tolerant. Plant out after the chance of frost has passed.

Tips

Added to an annual or mixed border, angelonia looks most attractive when planted in groups. It is also well suited to a pondside or streamside planting.

Recommended

A. angustifolia is a bushy, upright plant with loose spikes of flowers in varied shades of purple. Cultivars with white or bicolored flowers are available.

The individual flowers look a bit like orchid blossoms, but angelonia is actually in the same family as snapdragon.

Also called: angel wings, summer snapdragon **Features:** attractive flowers
Flower color: purple, blue, white, bicolored
Height: 12–24" **Spread:** 12"

Bacopa
Sutera

Bacopa snuggles under and around the stems of taller plants, forming a dense carpet dotted with tiny, white to pale lavender flowers, and eventually drifting over pot edges to form a waterfall of stars.

Growing

Bacopa grows well in **partial shade** with protection from the hot afternoon sun. The soil should be of **average fertility, humus rich, moist** and **well drained**. Don't allow this plant to dry out or the leaves will quickly die. Cutting back dead growth may encourage new shoots to form.

Tips

Bacopa is a popular plant for hanging baskets, mixed containers and window boxes. It is not recommended as a bedding plant because it fizzles quickly when the weather gets hot, particularly if you forget to water. Plant bacopa where you will see it every day so you will remember to water it.

S. cordata (above & below)

Bacopa is a perennial that is grown as an annual outdoors. It will thrive as a houseplant in a bright room.

Recommended

S. cordata is a compact, trailing plant that bears small, white flowers all summer. Cultivars with larger, white flowers, lavender flowers, or gold and green variegated foliage are available.

Features: decorative flowers; foliage; habit
Flower color: white, lavender **Height:** 3–6"
Spread: 12–20"

Begonia
Begonia

With their beautiful flowers, compact habit and decorative foliage, begonia are sure to fulfill your shade-gardening needs.

Growing
Light or partial shade is best for this plant, though some wax begonias tolerate sun if their soil is kept moist. The soil should be **fertile, rich in organic matter** and **well drained** with a **neutral or acidic pH**. Allow the soil to dry out slightly between waterings, particularly for tuberous begonias.

Begonias love warm weather, so don't plant them out before the soil warms in spring. If they sit in cold soil, they may become stunted and fail to thrive.

Tips
All begonias are useful for shaded garden beds and planters. The trailing, tuberous varieties can be used in hanging baskets and along rock walls where the flowers will cascade over the edges.

Wax begonias have a neat, rounded habit that makes them particularly attractive as edging plants. Rex begonias, with their dramatic foliage, are useful as specimen plants in containers and beds.

Recommended
B. **Rex Cultorum Hybrids** (rex begonias) are grown for their dramatic, colorful foliage.

Wax begonias are ideal flowers for the lazy gardener because they are generally pest free and bloom all summer, even without deadheading.

B. Rex Cultorum hybrid (above),
B. x *tuberhybrida* (below)

B. semperflorens (wax begonias) have pink, white, red or bicolored flowers and green, bronze, reddish or white-variegated foliage.

B. x tuberhybrida (tuberous begonias) are generally sold as tubers and are popular for their flowers that grow in many shades of red, pink, yellow, orange or white.

Features: colorful flowers; decorative foliage
Flower color: pink, white, red, yellow, orange, bicolored, picotee **Height:** 6–24"
Spread: 6–24"

Cleome

Cleome

C. hassleriana 'Royal Queen' (above), C. hassleriana (below)

Create a bold and exotic display in your garden with these lovely and unusual flowers.

Growing

Cleomes prefer **full sun** but tolerate partial shade. Plants adapt to **most soils**, though mixing in organic matter to help retain water is a good idea. These plants are drought tolerant but perform best when watered regularly. Pinch out the tip of the center stem on young plants to encourage branching and more blooms. Deadhead to prolong blooming and to reduce prolific self-seeding.

Tips

Cleomes can be planted in groups at the back of a border or in the center of an island bed. These striking plants also make an attractive addition to a large, mixed, container planting.

Recommended

C. hassleriana is a tall, upright plant with strong, supple, thorny stems. The foliage and flowers of this plant have a strong but not unpleasant scent. Flowers are borne in loose, rounded clusters at the ends of the leafy stems. Many cultivars are available.

C. serrulata (Rocky Mountain bee plant) is native to western North America but is rarely available commercially. The thornless, dwarf cultivar **'Solo'** is regularly available to be grown from seed and grows 12–18" tall with pink or white flowers.

Also called: spider flower **Features:** attractive, scented foliage and flowers; thorny stems **Flower color:** purple, pink, white **Height:** 1–5' **Spread:** 1–2'

Coleus

Solenostemon (Coleus)

here is a coleus for everyone. With foliage from brash yellows, oranges and reds to deep maroon and rose selections, the colors, textures and variations of coleus are almost limitless.

Growing

Coleus prefers to grow in **light or partial shade,** but it tolerates full shade if the shade isn't too dense, or full sun if the plants are watered regularly. The soil should be of **rich to average fertility, humus rich, moist** and **well drained**.

Place the seeds in a refrigerator for one or two days before planting them on the soil surface; the cold temperatures will assist in breaking the seeds' dormancy. They also need light to germinate. Seedlings will be green at first, but leaf variegation will develop as the plants mature.

Tips

The bold, colorful foliage makes a dramatic impact when the plants are grouped together as edging plants or in beds, borders or mixed containers. Coleus can also be grown indoors as a houseplant in a bright room.

When flower buds develop, it is best to pinch them off because the plants tend to stretch out and become less attractive after they flower.

S. scutellarioides cultivars (above & below)

Recommended

S. scutellarioides (*Coleus blumei* var. *verschaffeltii*) forms a bushy mound of foliage. The leaf edges range from slightly toothed to very ruffled. The leaves are usually multi-colored with shades ranging from pale greenish yellow to deep purple-black. Dozens of cultivars are available, but many cannot be started from seed.

Coleus can be trained to grow into a standard (tree) form by pinching off the side branches as the plant grows. Once the plant reaches the desired height, pinch from the top to encourage bushy growth.

Features: brightly colored foliage; insignificant flowers **Flower color:** light purple **Height:** 6–36" **Spread:** usually equal to height

Cosmos
Cosmos

C. bipinnatus (above & below)

With their array of bright shades, cosmos flowers add a splash of color to any garden.

Growing

Cosmos prefer **full sun in a sheltered location, out of the wind**. The soil should be of **poor or average fertility** and **well drained**. These plants are drought tolerant, so too much water or fertilizer can reduce flowering. Sow seed directly into the garden in spring. Deadhead to encourage more flowering. Poke twiggy sticks into the ground around young seedlings to support the plants as they grow.

Tips

Cosmos make an attractive addition to cottage gardens and the backs of borders. Try mass planting them in informal beds and borders.

Recommended

C. atrosanguineus (chocolate cosmos) is an upright plant that grows to 30" tall. It bears fragrant, dark maroon flowers that some claim smell a bit like chocolate.

C. bipinnatus is a tall plant with feathery foliage. It bears flowers in many shades of pink as well as red, purple or white. Older cultivars grow 3–6' tall, while some of the newer varieties grow 12–36" tall. Many cultivars are available.

C. sulphureus (yellow cosmos) is an upright plant that bears flowers in shades of yellow, orange or red. Older cultivars grow up to 7' tall, while newer ones grow 1–4' tall. Many cultivars are available.

Cosmos make lovely and long-lasting additions to cut-flower arrangements.

Features: flowers; feathery foliage
Flower color: pink, purple, red, white, yellow, orange, maroon **Height:** 1–7'
Spread: 12–18"

Dusty Miller

Senecio

S. *cineraria* 'Cirrus' (above), S. *cineraria* (below)

Dusty miller makes an artful addition to planters, window boxes and mixed borders, where the soft, silvery gray, deeply lobed foliage makes a good backdrop to show off the brightly colored flowers of other annuals.

Growing

Dusty miller prefers **full sun** but tolerates light shade. The soil should be of **average fertility** and **well drained**.

Tips

The soft, silvery, lacy leaves of this plant is its main feature. Dusty miller is used primarily as an edging plant, but it can also be used in beds, borders and containers.

Features: silvery foliage; neat habit
Flower color: yellow to cream (insignificant flowers); grown for foliage **Height:** 12–24" **Spread:** equal to height, or slightly narrower

Pinch off the flowers before they bloom. They aren't showy and they steal energy that could otherwise go to producing more foliage.

Recommended

S. cineraria forms a mound of fuzzy, silvery gray, lobed or finely divided foliage. Many cultivars have been developed with impressive foliage colors and shapes.

Mix dusty miller with geraniums, begonias or cockscombs to bring out the vibrant colors of those flowers.

Fan Flower

Scaevola

S. aemula (above & below)

Growing

Fan flower grows well in **full sun** or **light shade**. The soil should be of **average fertility, moist** and very **well drained**. Water regularly because this plant doesn't like to dry out completely. It does, however, recover quickly from wilting when watered.

Tips

Fan flower is popular for hanging baskets and containers, but it can also be used along the tops of rock walls and in rock gardens where it will trail down. This plant makes an interesting addition to mixed borders or it can be used under shrubs, where the long, trailing stems form an attractive groundcover.

Recommended

S. aemula forms a mound of foliage from which trailing stems emerge. The fan-shaped flowers come in shades of purple, usually with white bases. The species is rarely grown because there are many improved cultivars.

Fan flower's intriguing, one-sided flowers add interest to hanging baskets, planters and window boxes.

Given the right conditions, this Australian plant will flower abundantly from April through to frost.

Features: unique flowers; trailing habit
Flower color: blue, purple **Height:** up to 8" **Spread:** 36" or more

Floss Flower

Ageratum

A. houstonianum 'Hawaii Blue' (above), *A. houstonianum* (below)

The fluffy flowers, often in shades of blue, add softness and texture to the garden.

Growing

Floss flower prefers **full sun** but tolerates partial shade. The soil should be **fertile, moist** and **well drained**. A moisture-retaining mulch will prevent the soil from drying out excessively. Deadhead to prolong blooming and to keep plants looking tidy.

Tips

The smaller selections, which become almost completely covered in flowers, make excellent edging plants for flowerbeds and are attractive when grouped in masses or grown in planters. The taller selections can be included in the center of a flowerbed and are useful as cut flowers.

Recommended

A. houstonianum forms a large, leggy mound that can grow up to 24" tall, though many cultivars have been developed that have a low, bushy habit and generally grow about 12" tall. Flowers are produced in shades of blue, purple, pink or white.

Also called: ageratum **Features:** fuzzy flowers; mounded habit **Flower color:** blue, purple, pink, white **Height:** 6–36" **Spread:** 6–18"

Gazania

Gazania

G. *rigens* cultivars (above & below)

Few other flowers can rival gazania for adding vivid oranges, reds and yellows to the garden.

Growing

Gazania grows best in **full sun** but tolerates some shade. The soil should be of **poor to average fertility, sandy** and **well drained**. Gazania is drought tolerant and grows best when temperatures climb over 78° F. The flowers may only stay open on sunny days.

Tips

Low-growing gazania makes an excellent groundcover and is also useful on exposed slopes, in mixed containers and as an edging in flowerbeds. It is a wonderful plant for a xeriscape or dry garden design.

Recommended

G. rigens forms a low, basal rosette of lobed foliage. Large, daisy-like flowers with pointed petals are borne on strong stems above the plant. Many cultivars are available.

This native of southern Africa has very few pests and transplants easily, even when blooming.

Features: flowers **Flower color:** red, orange, yellow, pink, cream **Height:** usually 6–8"; may reach 12–18" **Spread:** 8–12"

Geranium

Pelargonium

*T*ough, predictable, sun loving and drought resistant, geraniums have earned their place as flowering favorites in the annual garden. If you are looking for something out of the ordinary, seek out the scented geraniums, with their fragrant and often decorative foliage.

Growing

Geraniums prefer **full sun** but tolerate partial shade, though they may not bloom as profusely. The soil should be **fertile** and **well drained**.

Deadheading is essential to keep geraniums blooming and looking neat.

Tips

Geraniums are very popular annual plants and can be used in borders, beds, planters, hanging baskets and window boxes.

Geraniums are perennials that are treated as annuals and can be kept indoors in a bright room for the winter.

Recommended

P. peltatum (ivy-leaved geranium) has thick, waxy leaves and a trailing habit. Many cultivars are available.

P. zonale (zonal geranium) is a bushy plant with red, pink, purple, orange or white flowers and,

P. peltatum cultivars (above & below)

frequently, banded or multi-colored foliage. Many cultivars are available.

P. **species** and **cultivars** (scented geraniums, scented pelargoniums) is a large group of geraniums that have scented leaves. The scents are grouped into the categories of rose, mint, citrus, fruit, spice and pungent.

Ivy-leaved geranium is one of the most beautiful plants to include in a mixed hanging basket.

Features: colorful flowers; decorative or scented foliage; variable habits
Flower color: red, pink, violet, orange, salmon, white, purple **Height:** 8–24"
Spread: 6–48"

Globe Amaranth
Gomphrena

Growing
Globe amaranth prefers **full sun**. The soil should be of **average fertility** and **well drained**. This plant is drought and heat tolerant and should only be watered during periods of extended drought. Soak seeds in water for two to four days to encourage sprouting before sowing into warm soil above 70° F.

Tips
Globe amaranth can be included in informal and cottage gardens as well as mixed beds and borders. Sometimes overlooked by gardeners because it doesn't start flowering until mid-summer, globe amaranth is worth including in the garden for the long-lasting color it provides from mid-summer to the first frost.

Recommended
G. globosa forms a rounded, bushy plant that grows 12–24" tall. It bears papery, clover-like flowers in shades of purple, magenta, white or pink. Many cultivars are available, including more compact selections.

G. globosa (above & below)

The flowerheads of globe amaranth are made up of brightly colored, papery bracts from which the tiny flowers emerge.

G. **'Strawberry Fields'** is a hybrid plant that bears bright orange-red or red flowers. It grows about 30" tall and spreads about 15".

Globe amaranth flowers are popular for cutting and drying. Harvest the blooms when they become round and plump; dry them upside down in a cool, dry location.

Features: flowers **Flower color:** purple, orange, magenta, pink, white, sometimes red **Height:** 6–30" **Spread:** 6–15"

Impatiens

Impatiens

Impatiens are the high-wattage darlings of the shade garden, delivering masses of flowers in a wide variety of colors.

Growing

Impatiens do best in **partial shade** or **light shade** but tolerate full shade or, if kept moist, full sun. New Guinea impatiens are the best adapted to sunny locations. The soil should be **fertile, humus rich, moist** and **well drained**.

Tips

Impatiens are known for their ability to grow and flower profusely, even in shade. Mass plant them in beds under trees, along shady fences or walls or in porch planters. They also look lovely in hanging baskets. New Guinea impatiens are grown as much for their variegated leaves as for their flowers.

Recommended

I. hawkeri (New Guinea hybrids, New Guinea impatiens) flowers in shades of red, orange, pink, purple or white. The foliage is often variegated with a yellow stripe down the center of each leaf.

I. walleriana (impatiens, busy Lizzie) flowers in shades of purple, red, burgundy, pink, yellow, salmon, orange, apricot or white and can be bicolored. Dozens of cultivars are available.

I. walleriana (above), *I. hawkeri* (below)

New impatiens varieties are introduced every year, expanding the selection of sizes, forms and colors for our gardens.

Features: colorful flowers; flowers well in shade **Flower color:** shades of purple, red, burgundy, pink, yellow, salmon, orange, apricot, white, bicolored
Height: 6–36" **Spread:** 12–24"

Lantana

Lantana

L. camara 'Spreading Sunset' (above & below)

These low-maintenance plants, with their stunning flowers, thrive in hot weather and won't suffer if you forget to water them.

Growing

Lantana grows best in **full sun** but tolerates partial shade. The soil should be **fertile, moist** and **well drained**. Plants are heat and drought tolerant. Cuttings can be taken in late summer and grown indoors for the winter so you will have plants the following summer.

Tips

Lantana is a tender shrub that is grown as an annual. It makes an attractive addition to beds and borders as well as in mixed containers and hanging baskets.

Recommended

L. camara is a bushy plant that bears round clusters of flowers in a variety of colors. The flowers often change color as they mature, giving flower clusters a striking, multi-colored appearance. Good examples of this are **'Feston Rose,'** which has flowers that open yellow and mature to bright pink, and **'Radiation,'** which bears flowers that open yellow and mature to red.

Also called: shrub verbena **Features:** stunning flowers **Flower color:** yellow, orange, pink, purple, red, white; often in combination **Height:** 18–24" **Spread:** up to 4'

Licorice Plant

Helichrysum

H. petiolare 'Silver' with verbena (above), *H. petiolare* 'Limelight' (below)

The silvery sheen of licorice plant is caused by a fine, soft pubescence on the leaves. It is a perfect complement to other plants, because silver is the ultimate blending color.

Growing

Licorice plant prefers **full sun**. The soil should be of **poor to average fertility, neutral or alkaline** and **well drained**. Licorice plant wilts when the soil dries but revives quickly once watered. If it outgrows its space, snip it back with a pair of pruners, shears or even scissors.

Tips

Licorice plant is a perennial that is grown as an annual, and it is prized for its foliage rather than its flowers.

Include it in your hanging baskets, planters and window boxes to provide a soft, silvery backdrop for the colorful flowers of other plants. Licorice plant can also be used as a groundcover in beds, borders, rock gardens and along the tops of retaining walls.

Recommended

H. petiolare is a trailing plant with fuzzy, gray-green leaves. Cultivars are more common than the species and include varieties with lime green, silver or variegated leaves.

Licorice plant is a good indicator plant for hanging baskets—when you notice licorice plant looking wilted, it is time to water your baskets.

Features: trailing habit; colorful, fuzzy foliage **Flower color:** grown for foliage **Height:** 20" **Spread:** about 36"; sometimes up to 6'

Million Bells

Calibrachoa

'Trailing Blue' (above), 'Trailing Pink' (below)

Million bells is charming, and given the right conditions, blooms continually during the growing season.

Growing

Million bells prefers **full sun**. The soil should be **fertile, moist** and **well drained**. Although it prefers to be watered regularly, million bells is fairly drought resistant once established.

Million bells blooms well into autumn; it becomes hardier over summer and as the weather cools.

Tips

Popular for planters and hanging baskets, million bells is also attractive in beds and borders. It grows all summer and needs plenty of room to spread or it will overtake other flowers. Pinch back to keep the plants compact.

Recommended

Calibrachoa **Hybrids** have a dense, trailing habit. They bear small flowers that look like petunias. The **Superbells Series** is noted for superior disease resistance and a wide range of uniquely colored flowers.

Also called: calibrachoa, trailing petunia
Features: colorful flowers; trailing habit
Flower color: pink, purple, yellow, red-orange, white, blue **Height:** 6–12"
Spread: up to 24"

Nasturtium

Tropaeolum

These fast-growing, brightly colored flowers are easy to grow, making them popular with beginning and experienced gardeners alike.

Growing

Nasturtiums prefer **full sun** but tolerate some shade. The soil should be of **poor to average fertility, light, moist** and **well drained**. Soil that is too rich or has too much nitrogen fertilizer will result in a lot of leaves and very few flowers. Allow the soil to drain completely between waterings. Sow directly in the garden once the danger of frost has passed.

Tips

Nasturtiums are used in beds, borders, containers and hanging baskets and on sloped banks. The climbing varieties can be grown up trellises or over rock walls or places that need concealing. These plants thrive in poor locations, and they make an interesting addition to plantings on hard-to-mow slopes.

The leaves and flowers are edible, adding a peppery flavor to salads.

T. majus (above), *T. majus* 'Alaska' (below)

Recommended

T. majus has a trailing habit, but many of the cultivars have bushier, more refined habits. Cultivars offer differing flower colors or variegated foliage.

Features: brightly colored flowers; attractive leaves; edible leaves and flowers; varied habits **Flower color:** red, orange, yellow, burgundy, pink, cream, gold, white, bicolored **Height:** 12–18" for dwarf varieties; up to 10' for trailing varieties **Spread:** equal to height

Nemesia
Nemesia

N. strumosa 'Joan Wilder' (above & below)

This plant, with its attractive, colorful flowers, is another of the many popular floral introductions from South Africa.

Growing
Nemesias prefer **full sun**. The soil should be **average to fertile, slightly acidic, moist** and **well drained**. Regular watering will keep these plants blooming through summer.

Tips
Nemesias make a bright and colorful addition to the front of a mixed border or mixed container planting.

Recommended
N. strumosa forms a bushy mound of bright green foliage, with flowers in shades of blue, purple, pink, red, orange, yellow or white, and often bicolored. The more heat-tolerant cultivars include **'Sunsatia Coconut,'** **'Peach'** and the **Safari Series**.

Combine the blue and white flowers of 'Blue Bird' with the red and white flowers of 'Cranberry' and celebrate the Fourth of July all summer.

Features: bushy plants; flowers **Flower color:** blue, purple, pink, red, yellow, orange, white, bicolored **Height:** 6–24" **Spread:** 4–12"

Nicotiana

Nicotiana

Nicotianas were originally cultivated for the wonderful fragrance of their flowers, a feature that, in some cases, has been lost in favor of more flower colors. However, fragrant varieties are still available.

Growing

Nicotianas grow equally well in **full sun, light shade** or **partial shade**. The soil should be **fertile, high in organic matter, moist** and **well drained**. They tolerate light fall frosts. Nicotianas tend to self-seed; young seedlings can be transplanted as desired.

Tips

Nicotianas are popular in beds and borders, creating dramatic backdrops and delicately filling spaces. They can also be used as edging plants, depending on the selection. All nicotianas do well in containers, but the dwarf varieties are best suited. Do not plant nicotianas near tomatoes because, as members of the same plant family, they share a vulnerability to many of the same diseases.

Recommended

N. langsdorfii bears delicate, airy clusters of lime green, trumpet-shaped flowers on plants that grow 3–5' tall.

N. x sanderae (*N. alata* x *N. forgetiana*) is a hybrid from which many bushy cultivars with showy, brightly colored flowers have been developed.

N. sylvestris with N. x sanderae cultivars (above),
N. x sanderae cultivar (below)

N. sylvestris grows up to 4' tall with bright green leaves and terminal clusters of pendulous, fragrant, white flowers.

Nicotiana flowers are most fragrant in the evening, with N. sylvestris having the most captivating scent.

Also called: flowering tobacco plant
Features: fragrant or colorful flowers
Flower color: red, pink, green, yellow, white, purple **Height:** 12–60" **Spread:** 12"

Osteospermum
Osteospermum

O. ecklonis Starwhirls Series (above), O. ecklonis (below)

Because of osteospermum's dislike of hot weather, it may be best to use these attractive daisies to add a bright splash of color in late summer and fall when we most need it.

Growing

Osteospermum grows best in **full sun**. The soil should be of **average fertility, moist** and **well drained**. Don't let plants dry out enough to wilt but avoid overwatering as well. An organic mulch will keep the soil moist and reduce the need for watering. Dead-head to prolong flowering and to keep plants looking neat. Pinch young plants to encourage bushy growth.

Tips

Osteospermum makes a bright addition to mixed container plantings and can be included in beds and borders. Late summer plantings will flower until the first heavy frost.

Recommended

O. ecklonis is a subshrub with a variable habit, ranging from quite upright in form to a more prostrate habit. Cultivars in the **Symphony Series** and **Soprano Series** are noted for improved heat tolerance.

You may find these plants listed as both Osteospermum *and* Dimorphotheca. *The latter is a closely related genus that used to include the species now listed as* Osteospermum.

Also called: African daisy, Cape daisy **Features:** attractive flowers, often with contrasting centers **Flower color:** shades of orange, peach, yellow, pink, purple, lavender, white; often with contrasting, dark blue or purple centers **Height:** 10–20" **Spread:** 10–20"

Petunia

Petunia

For speedy growth, prolific blooming, ease of care and a huge variety of selections, petunias are hard to beat.

Growing

Petunias prefer **full sun**. The soil should be of **average to rich fertility, light, sandy** and **well drained**. Pinch halfway back in mid-summer to keep plants bushy and to encourage new growth and flowers.

Tips

Use petunias in beds, borders, containers and hanging baskets.

Recommended

P. x *hybrida* is a large group of popular, sun-loving annuals that fall into three categories: **grandifloras** have the largest flowers in the widest range of colors, but they can be damaged by rain; **multifloras** bear more flowers that are smaller and less easily damaged by heavy rain; and **millifloras** have the smallest flowers in the narrowest range of colors, but this type is the most prolific and least likely to be damaged by heavy rain. Cultivars of all types are available and new selections are made available almost every year.

Multiflora-type 'Tidal Wave Silver' (above), Multiflora-type cultivar (below)

These hybrid series bloom continuously, spread vigorously and grow densely. They tolerate wet weather and offer tremendous options for hanging baskets, containers and borders.

Features: colorful flowers; versatile plants
Flower color: pink, purple, red, white, yellow, coral, blue, bicolored **Height:** 6–18" **Spread:** 12–24" or wider

Salvia
Salvia

S. *farinacea* and S. *splendens* (above), S, *riridis* (below)

Salvias should be part of every annual garden—the attractive and varied forms have something to offer every style of garden.

Growing

All salvia plants prefer **full sun** but tolerate light shade. The soil should be **moist** and **well drained** and of **average to rich fertility,** with a lot of **organic matter.**

Tips

Salvias look good grouped in beds and borders and in containers. The flowers are long lasting and make good cut flowers for arrangements.

To keep plants producing flowers, water often and fertilize monthly.

Recommended

S. argentea (silver sage) is grown for its large, fuzzy, silvery leaves. *S. coccinea* (Texas sage) is a bushy, upright plant that bears whorled spikes of white, pink, blue or purple flowers. *S. farinacea* (mealy cup sage, blue sage) has bright blue flowers clustered along stems powdered with silver. Cultivars are available. *S. splendens* (salvia, scarlet sage) is grown for its spikes of bright red, tubular flowers. Recently, cultivars have become available in white, pink, purple or orange. *S. viridis* (*S. horminium;* annual clary sage) is grown for its colorful pink, purple, blue or white bracts, not for its flowers.

With over 900 species of Salvia, *you're sure to find one you'll like for your garden.*

Also called: sage **Features:** colorful summer flowers; attractive foliage **Flower color:** red, blue, purple, burgundy, pink, orange, salmon, yellow, cream, white, bicolored **Height:** 8–48" **Spread:** 8–48"

Sweet Potato Vine

Ipomoea

'Blackie' (above), 'Margarita' (below)

his vigorous, rambling plant with lime green, bruised purple or green, pink and cream variegated leaves can make any gardener look like a genius.

Growing

Grow sweet potato vine in **full sun**. Any type of soil will do but a **light, well-drained** soil of **poor fertility** is preferred.

Tips

Sweet potato vine is a great addition to mixed planters, window boxes and hanging baskets. In a rock garden it will scramble about, and along the top of a retaining wall it will cascade over the edge.

Although this plant is a vine, its bushy habit and colorful leaves make it a useful foliage plant.

Recommended

I. batatas (sweet potato vine) is a twining climber that is grown for its attractive foliage rather than its flowers. Cultivars come in a wide variety of leaf colors.

As a bonus, when you pull up your plant at the end of summer, you can eat any tubers (sweet potatoes) that have formed.

Features: decorative foliage **Flower color:** grown for foliage **Height:** about 12" **Spread:** up to 10'

Verbena

Verbena

V. bonariensis (above), *V. x hybrida* (below)

Verbenas offer butterflies a banquet. Butterfly visitors include tiger swallowtails, silver-spotted skippers, great spangled fritillaries and painted ladies.

Growing

Verbenas grow best in **full sun**. The soil should be **fertile** and **very well drained**. Pinch back young plants for bushy growth.

Tips

Use verbenas on rock walls and in beds, borders, rock gardens, containers, hanging baskets and window

boxes. They make good substitutes for ivy-leaved geranium where the sun is hot and where a roof overhang keeps the mildew-prone verbenas dry.

Recommended

V. bonariensis forms a low clump of foliage from which tall, stiff stems bear clusters of small, purple flowers. This plant is excellent when combined with ornamental grasses.

V. x hybrida (garden verbena) is a bushy plant that may be upright or spreading. It bears clusters of small flowers in a wide range of colors. Superior cultivars can be found sold under the **Babylon, Superbina, Temari** and **Tukana Series** names.

The Romans, it is said, believed verbena could rekindle the flames of dying love. They named it Herba Veneris *or 'plant of Venus.'*

Features: flowers **Flower color:** red, pink, purple, blue, yellow, scarlet, silver, peach, white; some with white centers **Height:** 8–60" **Spread:** 12–36"

Zinnia

Zinnia

innias are popular in gardens and flower arrangements, adding much needed color to the late-summer and fall garden.

Growing

Zinnias grow best in **full sun.** The soil should be **fertile, rich in organic matter, moist** and **well drained**. To avoid disturbing the roots when transplanting seedlings, start seeds in individual peat pots. Deadhead to prolong blooming and to keep plants looking neat.

Tips

Zinnias are useful in beds, borders, containers and cutting gardens. The dwarf selections can be used as edging plants. These plants provide wonderful fall color.

Recommended

Z. angustifolia (narrow-leaf zinnia) is a low, mounding, mildew-resistant plant that bears yellow, orange or white flowers. It grows to about 8" tall. Cultivars are available.

Z. elegans is a bushy, upright plant with daisy-like flowers in a variety of forms. Heights vary from 6–36". Many cultivars are available.

Z. haageana (Mexican zinnia) is a bushy plant with narrow leaves that bears bright bicolored or tricolored, daisy-like flowers in shades of orange, red, yellow, maroon, brown or gold. Plants grow 12–24" tall. Cultivars are available.

Z. haageana 'Orange Star' (above), *Z. elegans* mixed cultivars (below)

Mildew can be a problem for zinnias, so choose mildew-resistant cultivars and grow them in locations with good air circulation.

Features: bushy plants; colorful flowers
Flower color: shades of red, yellow, green, purple, orange, pink, white, maroon, brown, gold; some are bicolored or tricolored
Height: 8–36" **Spread:** 12"

Aster

Aster (Symphyotrichum)

A. *novi-belgii* cultivars (above & below)

Growing

Asters prefer **full sun** but tolerate partial shade. The soil should be **fertile, moist** and **well drained**. Pinch or shear these plants back in early summer to promote dense growth and to reduce disease problems. Mulch in winter to protect plants from temperature fluctuations. Divide every two or three years to maintain vigor and control spread.

Tips

Use asters in the middle of borders and in cottage gardens, or naturalize them in wild gardens.

Recommended

Some *Aster* species have recently been reclassified under the genus *Symphyotrichum.* You may see both names at garden centers.

A. dumosus (Michaelmas daisy, New York aster) is a dense, mounded plant available in a wide array of colors.

A. novae-angliae (Michaelmas daisy, New England aster) is an upright, spreading, clump-forming perennial that bears purple, yellow-centered flowers. Many cultivars are available.

A. novi-belgii (Michaelmas daisy, New York aster) is a dense, upright, clump-forming perennial with purple flowers. Many cultivars are available.

Asters are among the final plants to bloom before the snow flies; their purples and pinks contrast well with the yellow-flowered perennials common in the late-summer and fall garden.

Features: late summer to mid-autumn flowers **Flower color:** red, white, blue, purple, pink; often with yellow centers **Height:** 10–60" **Spread:** 18–36" **Hardiness:** zones 3–8

Astilbe
Astilbe

Astilbes are beacons in the shade. Their high-impact flowers will brighten any gloomy section of your garden.

Growing

Astilbes grow best in **light or partial shade** but tolerate full shade, though they will not flower as much in full shade. The soil should be **fertile, humus rich, acidic, moist** and **well drained**. Although astilbes appreciate moist soil, they don't like standing water.

Astilbes should be divided every three years or so to maintain plant vigor. Root masses may lift out of the soil as they mature; add a layer of topsoil and mulch if this occurs.

Tips

Astilbes can be grown near the edges of bog gardens and ponds and in woodland gardens and shaded borders.

Recommended

There are many species, hybrids and cultivars of astilbe available. In general, these plants form bushy clumps of leaves and bear plumes of colorful flowers. The following are a few popular selections. *A.* x *arendsii* is a group of

In late summer, transplant seedlings found near the parent plant to create plumes of color all through the garden.

A. x *arendsii* cultivar (above),
A. x *arendsii* 'Bressingham Beauty' (below)

hybrids with many available cultivars, including **'Avalanche'** with white flowers, **'Bressingham Beauty'** with pink flowers and **'Fanal'** with red flowers. *A. chinensis* var. *pumila* is a dense, vigorous, low-growing, spreading perennial that tolerates dry soil better than other astilbe species. *A. japonica* is a compact, clump-forming perennial. The species is rarely grown in favor of the many cultivars, including **'Deutschland'** with white flowers and **'Peach Blossom'** with peachy pink flowers.

Features: attractive foliage; summer flowers **Flower color:** white, pink, purple, peach, red **Height:** 10–48" **Spread:** 8–36" **Hardiness:** zones 3–9

Balloon Flower

Platycodon

P. grandiflorus (above & below)

Growing

Balloon flower grows well in **full sun** or **partial shade**. The soil should be **average to fertile, light, moist** and **well drained**. This plant dislikes too wet a soil. The roots resent being disturbed so this plant should not need dividing. Shoots that sprout up around the plant can be gently removed and planted to propagate. Deadhead to prolong blooming and to keep plants looking neat.

Tips

Use balloon flower in borders, rock gardens and cottage gardens. It does not like being crowded by other plants so give it plenty of room to spread.

Balloon flower sprouts fairly late in spring. Mark the location where it is growing in fall so you will avoid disturbing it in spring.

Recommended

P. grandiflorus is an upright, clump-forming perennial that grows 24–36" tall and spreads 12–18". It bears blue or purple flowers in summer. Cultivars tend to be lower-growing and bushier in habit and may have white, pink, blue, purple or double flowers.

Children and adults find the temptation to gently squeeze open the rounded, balloon-like buds hard to resist.

When using these lovely flowers in arrangements, singe the cut ends with a lit match to prevent the milky white sap from running.

Features: habit; summer flowers; attractive flower buds **Flower color:** blue, purple, pink, white **Height:** 12–36" **Spread:** 12–18" **Hardiness:** zones 3–8

Bellflower

Campanula

Thanks to their wide range of heights and habits, it is possible to plant bellflowers almost anywhere in the garden.

Growing

Bellflowers grow well in **full sun, partial shade** or **light shade**. The soil should be of **average to high fertility** and **well drained**. These plants appreciate a mulch to keep their roots cool and moist in summer and protected in winter, particularly if snow cover is inconsistent. Deadhead to prolong blooming.

Tips

Plant upright and mounding bellflowers in borders and cottage gardens. Use low, spreading and trailing bellflowers in rock gardens and on rock walls. You can also edge beds with the low-growing varieties.

Recommended

C. x **'Birch Hybrid'** is a low-growing and spreading plant. It bears light blue to mauve flowers in summer.

C. carpatica (Carpathian bellflower, Carpathian harebell) is a spreading, mounding perennial that bears blue, white or purple flowers in summer. Several cultivars are available.

C. glomerata (clustered bellflower) forms a clump of upright stems and bears clusters of purple, blue or white flowers throughout most of the summer season.

C. persicifolia (above),
C. carpatica 'White Clips' (below)

C. persicifolia (peach-leaved bellflower) is an upright perennial that bears white, blue or purple flowers from early summer to mid-summer.

C. poscharskyana (Serbian bellflower) is a trailing perennial that likes to wind its way around other plants. It bears light, violet-blue flowers in summer and early autumn.

Also called: campanula **Features:** spring, summer or autumn flowers; varied growing habits **Flower color:** blue, white, purple, pink **Height:** 4–72" **Spread:** 12–36" **Hardiness:** zones 3–7

Blazing Star

Liatris

L. spicata 'Kobold' (above), *L. spicata* (below)

Blazing star is an outstanding cut flower with fuzzy, spiked blossoms above grass-like foliage. It is also an excellent plant for attracting butterflies to the garden.

Growing

Blazing star prefers **full sun**. The soil should be of **average fertility, sandy** and **humus rich**. Water well during the growing season but don't allow the plants to stand in water during cool weather. Mulch during summer to prevent moisture loss.

Trim off the spent flower spikes to promote a longer blooming period and to keep blazing star looking tidy. Divide every three or four years in autumn. The clump will appear crowded when it is time to divide.

Tips

Use blazing star in borders and meadow plantings. Plant it in a location that has good drainage to avoid root rot in winter. Blazing star also grows well in planters.

Recommended

L. spicata is a clump-forming, erect plant. The flowers are pinkish purple or white. Several cultivars are available.

Also called: spike gayfeather, gayfeather
Features: summer flowers; grass-like foliage
Flower color: purple, white   **Height:** 18–36"
Spread: 18–24"   **Hardiness:** zones 3–9

Bleeding Heart
Dicentra

Every garden should have a bleeding heart. Tucked away in a shady spot, this lovely plant appears in spring and fills the garden with fresh promise.

Growing

Bleeding hearts prefer **light shade** but tolerate partial or full shade. The soil should be **humus rich, moist** and **well drained**. Very dry summer conditions cause the plants to die back, though they will revive in autumn or the following spring. Bleeding hearts must remain moist while blooming in order to prolong the flowering period. Regular watering will keep the flowers coming until midsummer. *D. eximia* and *D. spectabilis* rarely need dividing. *D. formosa* can be divided every three years or so.

Tips

Bleeding hearts can be naturalized in a woodland garden or grown in a border or rock garden. They make excellent early-season specimen plants and do well near ponds or streams.

Recommended

D. eximia (fringed bleeding heart) forms a loose, mounded clump of lacy, fern-like foliage and bears pink or white flowers in spring and sporadically over summer.

D. formosa (above), *D. spectabilis* (below)

D. formosa (western bleeding heart) is a low-growing, wide-spreading plant with pink flowers that fade to white as they mature. The most drought tolerant of the bleeding hearts, this species is the most likely to continue flowering all summer.

D. spectabilis (common bleeding heart, Japanese bleeding heart) forms a large, elegant mound that bears flowers with white inner petals and pink outer petals. Several cultivars are available.

All bleeding hearts contain toxic alkaloids, and some people develop allergic skin reactions from contact with these plants.

Features: spring and summer flowers; attractive foliage **Flower color:** pink, white, red, purple **Height:** 12–48"
Spread: 12–36" **Hardiness:** zones 3–9

Brunnera
Brunnera

These beautiful, shade-loving plants are a welcome addition to any garden. The variegated selections bring light to corners of the garden that might otherwise seem dark.

Growing

Brunnera grows best in **light shade** but will grow in partial shade with morning sun if the soil is kept consistently moist. The soil should be of **average fertility, humus rich, moist** and **well drained**. The species and its cultivars do not tolerate drought. Cut back faded foliage in mid-summer to encourage a flush of new growth.

Tips

Brunnera makes a great addition to a woodland or shaded garden. Its low, bushy habit makes it useful as a ground-cover or as an addition to a shaded border.

Recommended

B. macrophylla forms a mound of soft, heart-shaped leaves and produces loose clusters of blue flowers all spring. Cultivars with silver- or cream-variegated foliage are available.

B. macrophylla 'Jack Frost' in mixed container (above),
B. macrophylla 'Dawson's White' (below)

Brunnera is related to borage and forget-me-nots and rarely suffers from any problems.

Also called: Siberian bugloss **Features:** spring flowers; attractive foliage **Flower color:** blue **Height:** 12–18" **Spread:** 18–24" **Hardiness:** zones 3–8

Cardinal Flower

Lobelia

The brilliant red of these flowers is motivation enough for some gardeners to install a pond or bog garden, just to meet cardinal flowers' moist soil requirements.

Growing

Cardinal flowers grow well in **full sun, light shade** or **partial shade**. The soil should be **fertile, slightly acidic** and **moist**. Avoid letting the soil dry out completely, especially in a sunny location. Mulch plants lightly in winter for protection. Deadhead to keep the plants neat and to encourage a possible second flush of blooms. Plants tend to self-seed, but seedlings may not be identical to parent plants. Seedlings can be moved to new locations or they can be left where they are to replace the short-lived parent plants when they die.

Tips

These plants are best suited to streamside or pondside plantings or in bog gardens. They can also be included in moist beds and borders or in any location where they will be watered regularly.

Recommended

L. cardinalis forms an upright clump of bronze-green leaves and bears spikes of bright red

L. cardinalis (above & below)

flowers from summer to fall. There are also many hybrids and cultivars available, often with flowers in shades of blue, purple, red or pink. Some hybrids and cultivars are as hardy as the species while others are not as hardy.

These lovely members of the bellflower family contain deadly alkaloids and have poisoned people who tried to use them in herbal medicines.

Features: summer flowers; bronze-green foliage **Flower color:** bright red, purple, blue, pink **Height:** 24–48" **Spread:** 12–24" **Hardiness:** zones 4–9

Catmint

Nepeta

N. x faassenii (above & below)

Catmint is an easy-to-grow perennial that provides a wonderful show of flowers all summer long.

Growing

Catmint grows well in **full sun** or **partial shade**. The soil should be of **average fertility** and **well drained**. Plants tend to flop over in too fertile a soil. Pinch plants back in early June to encourage bushy, compact growth. Cut back after blooming to encourage a second flush of flowers.

Cats are attracted to the related plant catnip (N. cataria); you may find that cats are drawn to your garden if you grow catmint.

Tips

The lower-growing catmints can be used to edge borders and pathways and can also be used in rock gardens. Taller selections make lovely additions to perennial beds. All catmints work well in herb gardens and with roses in a cottage garden.

Recommended

N. x faassenii forms a clump of upright and spreading stems. Spikes of blue or lavender flowers are produced in spring and summer and sometimes again in fall. Many cultivars and hybrids are available.

Features: spring or summer flowers; habit; fragrant foliage **Flower color:** blue, purple, pink, white **Height:** 18–36" **Spread:** 18–36" **Hardiness:** zones 3–8

Chrysanthemum

Chrysanthemum

*P*erk up your fall garden with a bright display of fall 'mums' with their masses of colorful flowers.

Growing

Chrysanthemums grow best in **full sun**. The soil should be **fertile, moist** and **well drained**. Plant as early in the growing season as possible to increase the chances that chrysanthemums will survive winter. Pinch plants back in early summer to encourage bushy growth and to increase flower production. Divide plants every two or three years to keep them growing vigorously.

Tips

Chrysanthemums provide a blaze of color in the fall garden that lasts until the first hard frost. In groups, or as specimen plants, they can be included in borders, in planters or in plantings close to the house. Purchased in fall, they can be added to spots where summer annuals have faded.

Recommended

C. **hybrids** form a diverse group of plants with varied hardiness in Michigan. A few popular hybrids are *C.* **'Mei-Kyo,'** a vigorous grower that produces deep pink flowers in mid- to late October and the *C.* **'Prophet'**

series that has cultivars with flowers in a wide range of colors, including **'Christine'** with deep, salmon pink flowers and **'Raquel'** with bright red flowers.

Although the name Chrysanthemum comes from the Greek and means 'golden flower,' these plants actually bloom in a wide range of bright colors.

Features: late-summer or fall flowers; habit
Flower color: orange, yellow, pink, red, purple **Height:** 12–36" **Spread:** 24–48"
Hardiness: zones 5–9

Coreopsis
Coreopsis

C. verticillata 'Moonbeam' (above), C. verticillata (below)

These plants produce flowers all summer and are easy to grow; they make a fabulous addition to every garden.

Mass plant coreopsis to fill in a dry, exposed bank where nothing else will grow, and enjoy the bright, sunny flowers all summer long.

Growing

Coreopsis grows best in **full sun**. The soil should be of **average fertility, sandy, light** and **well drained**. Plants can develop crown rot in moist, cool locations with heavy soil. Too fertile a soil will encourage floppy growth. Deadhead to keep plants blooming.

Tips

Coreopsis are versatile plants, useful in formal and informal borders and in meadow plantings and cottage gardens. They look best when planted in groups.

Recommended

C. auriculata 'Nana' (mouse-eared tickseed) is a low-growing species, well suited to rock gardens and the fronts of borders. It grows about 12" tall and spreads indefinitely, though slowly. It bears yellow-orange flowers in late spring.

C. verticillata (thread-leaf coreopsis) is a mound-forming plant with attractive, finely divided foliage and bright yellow flowers. It grows 24–32" tall and spreads 18". Available cultivars include 'Moonbeam,' which forms a mound of delicate, lacy foliage and bears creamy yellow flowers.

Also called: tickseed **Features:** summer flowers; attractive foliage **Flower color:** yellow, orange **Height:** 12–32" **Spread:** 12–24" **Hardiness:** zones 3–9

Daylily
Hemerocallis

The daylily's adaptability and durability combined with its variety in color, blooming period, size and texture explain this perennial's popularity.

Growing

Daylilies grow in any light from **full sun to full shade**. The deeper the shade, the fewer flowers will be produced. The soil should be **fertile, moist** and **well drained,** but these plants adapt to most conditions and are hard to kill once established. Divide every two or three years to keep plants vigorous and to propagate them. They can, however, be left indefinitely without dividing. Deadhead to prolong the blooming period.

Be careful when deadheading purple-flowered daylilies because the sap can stain fingers and clothes.

Tips

Plant daylilies alone, or group them in borders, on banks and in ditches to control erosion. They can be naturalized in woodland or meadow gardens. Small varieties are also nice in planters.

'Dewey Roquemore' (above), 'Bonanza' (below)

Recommended

Daylilies come in an almost infinite number of forms, sizes and colors in a range of species, cultivars and hybrids. Visit your local garden center or daylily grower to find out what's available and most suitable for your garden.

Features: spring and summer flowers; grass-like foliage **Flower color:** every color, except blue and pure white **Height:** 12–48" **Spread:** 12–48" **Hardiness:** zones 2–8

False Indigo
Baptisia

Spikes of bright blue flowers in early summer and attractive green foliage make this plant a worthy addition, even if it does take up a sizeable amount of garden real estate.

Growing
False indigo prefers **full sun** but tolerates partial shade. However, too much shade causes lank growth that flops over easily. The soil should be of **poor to average fertility, sandy** and **well drained**.

False indigo has a strong tap root and resents being disturbed. It doesn't need dividing and can be left in one place for many years.

Tips
False indigo can be used in an informal border or a cottage garden. It is an attractive addition for a naturalized planting, on a slope, or in any sunny, well-drained spot in the garden.

Recommended
B. australis is an upright or somewhat spreading, clump-forming plant that bears spikes of purple-blue flowers in early summer.

B. australis (above & below)

If you've had difficulties growing lupines, try the far less demanding false indigo instead.

Features: late-spring or early-summer flowers; habit; foliage **Flower color:** purple-blue **Height:** 3–5' **Spread:** 2–4' **Hardiness:** zones 3–9

Foamflower
Tiarella

T. cordifolia (above & below)

Foamflowers form handsome groundcovers in shaded areas, with attractive leaves and delicate, starry, white flowers.

Growing

Foamflowers prefer **partial, light or full shade without afternoon sun**. The soil should be **humus rich, moist** and **slightly acidic,** though these plants adapt to most soils. Divide in spring. Deadhead to encourage re-blooming. If the foliage fades or rusts in summer, cut it partway to the ground and new growth will emerge.

These plants spread by underground stems, which are easily pulled up to stop excessive spread.

Tips

Foamflowers are excellent groundcovers for shaded and woodland gardens. They can be included in shaded borders and left to naturalize in wild gardens.

Recommended

T. cordifolia is a low-growing, spreading plant that bears spikes of foamy-looking, white flowers. Cultivars are available.

T. '**Maple Leaf**' is a clump-forming hybrid with bronze-green, maple-like leaves and pink-flushed flowers.

Features: spring and sometimes early-summer flowers; decorative foliage **Flower color:** white, pink **Height:** 4–12" **Spread:** 12–24" **Hardiness:** zones 3–8

Goat's Beard

Aruncus

A. dioicus (above & below)

Divide in spring or autumn. Use a sharp knife or an axe to cut the dense root mass into pieces. Fortunately, these plants rarely need dividing.

Tips

Goat's beard looks very natural growing near the sunny entrance or edge of a woodland garden, in a native plant garden or in a large, island planting. It may also be used in a border or alongside a stream or pond.

Recommended

A. aethusifolius (dwarf Korean goat's beard) forms a low-growing, compact mound and bears branched spikes of loosely held, cream flowers.

A. dioicus (giant goat's beard, common goat's beard) forms a large, bushy, shrub-like perennial with large plumes of creamy white flowers. There are several cultivars.

Despite its imposing size, goat's beard has a soft and delicate appearance with its divided foliage and large, plumy, cream flowers.

Growing

These plants prefer **partial to full shade**. If planted in deep shade, they bear fewer blooms. They tolerate some full sun as long as the soil is kept evenly moist and the plants are protected from the afternoon sun. The soil should be **fertile, moist** and **humus rich**.

Male and female flowers are produced on separate plants. In general, male flowers are full and fuzzy while female flowers are more pendulous, though it can be difficult to tell the difference.

Features: early to mid-summer blooms; shrub-like habit; attractive foliage and seed heads
Flower color: cream, white **Height:** 6–72"
Spread: 12–72" **Hardiness:** zones 3–8

Hardy Geranium

Geranium

There is a type of geranium that suits every garden, thanks to the beauty and diversity of this hardy plant.

Growing

Hardy geraniums grow well in **full sun, partial shade** or **light shade**. These plants dislike hot weather and prefer soil of **average fertility** and **good drainage**. *G. renardii* prefers a poor, well-drained soil. Divide the plants in spring.

G. *sanguineum* var. *striatum* (above),
G. *sanguineum* (below)

Tips

These long-flowering plants are great in a border; they fill in the spaces between shrubs and other larger plants, and keep the weeds down. Hardy geraniums can be included in rock gardens and woodland gardens, or mass planted as groundcovers.

Recommended

G. 'Brookside' is a clump-forming, drought-tolerant geranium with finely cut leaves and deep blue to violet-blue flowers.

G. macrorrhizum (bigroot geranium, scented cranesbill) forms a spreading mound of fragrant foliage and bears flowers in various shades of pink. Cultivars are available.

G. renardii (Renard's geranium) forms a clump of velvety, deeply veined, crinkled foliage. A few purple-veined, white flowers appear over summer, but the foliage is the main attraction.

G. sanguineum (bloodred cranesbill, bloody cranesbill) forms a dense, mounding clump and bears bright magenta flowers. Many cultivars are available.

If the foliage looks tatty in late summer, prune it back to rejuvenate it.

Also called: cranesbill geranium **Features:** spring or summer flowers; attractive, sometimes-fragrant foliage **Flower color:** white, red, pink, purple, blue **Height:** 4–36" **Spread:** 12–36" **Hardiness:** zones 3–8

Hellebore

Helleborus

H. orientalis (above)

These beautiful, spring-blooming groundcover plants are among the earliest harbingers of spring, providing the welcome sight of what's to come long before most other plants have even started to sprout.

All parts of hellebore are toxic, and the leaf edges can be sharp, so wear long sleeves and gloves when planting or dividing these plants.

Growing

Hellebores prefer **light, dappled shade** and a **sheltered location** but tolerate some direct sun if the soil stays evenly moist. The soil should be **fertile, humus rich, neutral to alkaline, moist** and **well drained**. Mulch plants in winter if they are in an exposed location. In a mild winter the leaves may stay evergreen and flowers may appear as early as February.

Tips

Use these plants in a sheltered border or rock garden, or naturalize in a woodland garden.

Recommended

H. x *hybridus* plants grow about 18" tall, with an equal spread. Plants may be deciduous or evergreen, and they bloom in a wide range of colors. Some cultivars have deeper-colored flowers, double flowers, spotted flowers or picotee flowers (with differently colored petal margins).

H. orientalis (lenten rose) is a clump-forming, evergreen perennial. It grows 12–24" tall with an equal spread. It bears white or greenish flowers that turn pink as they mature in mid- or late spring.

Also called: Lenten rose, Christmas rose
Features: late winter to mid-spring flowers
Flower color: white, green, pink, purple, yellow **Height:** 12–24" **Spread:** 12–24"
Hardiness: zones 5–9

Heuchera

Heuchera

From soft, yellow-greens and oranges to midnight purples and silver-dappled maroons, heucheras offer a great variety of foliage options for a perennial garden with partial shade.

Growing

Heucheras grow best in **light or partial shade**. The foliage colors can bleach out in full sun, and plants grow leggy in full shade. The soil should be of **average to rich fertility, humus rich, neutral to alkaline, moist** and **well drained. Good air circulation is essential**. Deadhead to prolong the bloom. Every two or three years, heucheras should be dug up and the oldest, woodiest roots and stems removed. Plants may be divided at this time, if desired, then replanted with the crown at or just above soil level.

Tips

Use heucheras as edging plants, in clusters and woodland gardens, or as groundcovers in low-traffic areas. Combine different foliage types for an interesting display.

Recommended

There are dozens of beautiful cultivars available with almost limitless variations of foliage markings and colors. See your local garden center or a mail-order catalog to discover what is available.

H. x *brizoides* 'Firefly' (above), *H. sanguinea* (below)

Heucheras have a strange habit of pushing themselves up out of the soil because of their shallow root systems. Mulch in autumn if the plants begin heaving from the ground.

Also called: coral bells, alum root
Features: very decorative foliage; spring or summer flowers **Flower color:** red, pink, white, yellow, purple **Height:** 12–48"
Spread: 6–18" **Hardiness:** zones 3–9

Hosta

Hosta

H. fortunei 'Francee' (above)

Breeders are always looking for new variations in hosta foliage. Swirls, stripes, puckers and ribs enhance the leaves' various sizes, shapes and colors.

Growing

Hostas prefer **light or partial shade** but will grow in full shade. Morning sun is preferable to afternoon sun in partial shade situations. The soil should ideally be **fertile, moist** and **well drained** but most soils are tolerated. Hostas are fairly drought tolerant, especially if given a mulch to help them retain moisture. Division is not required but can be done every few years in spring or summer to propagate new plants.

Tips

Hostas make wonderful woodland plants and look very attractive when combined with ferns and other fine-textured plants. Hostas are also good plants for a mixed border, particularly when used to hide the ugly, leggy, lower stems and branches of some shrubs. Hostas' dense growth and thick, shade-providing leaves allow them to suppress weeds.

Recommended

Hostas have been subjected to a great deal of crossbreeding and hybridizing, resulting in hundreds of cultivars. Visit your local garden center or get a mail-order catalog to find out what's available.

Some gardeners think the flowers clash with the foliage, and they remove the flower stems when they first emerge. If you find the flowers unattractive, removing them won't harm the plant.

Also called: plantain lily **Features:** decorative foliage; summer and autumn flowers **Flower color:** white, purple **Height:** 4–36" **Spread:** 6–72" **Hardiness:** zones 3–8

Iris

Iris

Irises are steeped in history and lore. Many say the flower color range of bearded irises approximates that of a rainbow.

Growing

Irises prefer **full sun** but tolerate very light or dappled shade. The soil should be of **average fertility** and **well drained**. Japanese iris and Siberian iris prefer a moist but still well-drained soil.

Divide in late summer or early autumn. When dividing bearded iris rhizomes, replant with the flat side of the foliage fan facing the garden. Dust the toe-shaped rhizome with a powder cleanser before planting to help prevent soft rot.

Deadhead irises to keep them tidy. Cut back the foliage of Siberian iris in spring.

Tips

All irises are popular border plants, but Japanese iris and Siberian iris are also useful alongside streams or ponds. Dwarf cultivars make attractive additions to rock gardens.

Wash your hands after handling irises because they can cause severe internal irritation if ingested. You may not want to plant them close to places where children like to play.

I. sibirica (above), *I. germanica* 'Stepping Out' (below)

Recommended

There are many iris species and hybrids available. Among the most popular is the bearded iris, often a hybrid of **I. germanica**. It has the widest range of flower colors but is susceptible to attack from the iris borer, which can kill a plant. Several irises are not susceptible, including **I. ensata** (Japanese iris) and **I. sibirica** (Siberian iris). Check with your local garden center to find out what's available.

Features: spring, summer and sometimes fall flowers; attractive foliage **Flower color:** pink, red, purple, blue, white, brown, yellow **Height:** 4–48" **Spread:** 6–48" **Hardiness:** zones 3–10

Japanese Anemone
Anemone

A. x hybrida (above), *A. x hybrida* 'Whirlwind' (below)

As the rest of the garden begins to fade in late summer, Japanese anemone is just beginning its fall show. The white and pink colors are a welcome sight in the fall garden that is usually dominated by yellow and orange.

Growing

Japanese anemone prefers **partial or light shade** but tolerates full sun. The soil should be of **average to high fertility, humus rich** and **moist**. Allow the soil to dry out when plants are dormant. Mulch the first winter to allow plants to become established.

Deadheading will keep plants tidy but will not prolong the blooming period.

Tips

Japanese anemones make a beautiful addition to lightly shaded borders, woodland gardens and cottage gardens.

Recommended

A. x hybrida is an upright plant with a suckering habit. Flowers in shades of pink or white are produced in late summer and early fall. Many cultivars are available.

The name windflower was given to describe the plumy seeds that are carried away on the wind.

Also called: windflower **Features:** late summer to fall flowers; attractive foliage **Flower color:** pink, white **Height:** 2–5' **Spread:** 2' **Hardiness:** zones 5–9

Ligularia

Ligularia

Brighten up a shaded spot in your garden with these impressive plants and their bright yellow flowers.

Growing

Ligularia prefers **light shade** or **partial shade** with **protection from the afternoon sun**. The soil should be of **average fertility, humus rich** and **consistently moist**. The leaves tend to wilt in hot sun, even when the soil is moist. They will revive at night, but this won't help their droopy appearance during the day. If your ligularia looks wilted, it is best to move the plant to a cooler, more shaded position in the garden.

L. dentata (above & below)

Tips

Use ligularias alongside a pond or stream. They can also be used in a well-watered border or naturalized in a moist meadow or woodland garden.

Recommended

L. dentata (bigleaf ligularia, golden groundsel) forms a clump of rounded, heart-shaped leaves. It grows 3–5' tall and spreads 3–4'. In summer and early fall it bears clusters of orange-yellow flowers that are held above the foliage. Cultivars are available.

L. stenocephala (narrow-spiked ligularia) has toothed foliage and bears bright yellow flowers on dark, purple-green spikes. It grows 3–5' tall, with an equal spread. The most common cultivar is **'The Rocket,'** with coarsely toothed, heart-shaped foliage and purple veins near the leaf bases.

If you are finding it difficult to keep your soil moist enough for these plants to thrive, you may try lining a large planting hole with an old sheet of plastic so that water drains more slowly away from the roots.

Features: summer or early-fall flowers; foliage **Flower color:** yellow, orange **Height:** 3–5' **Spread:** 3–5' **Hardiness:** zones 4–9

Loosestrife

Lysimachia

L. nummularia

Loosestrife is a lovely, low-growing, ground-covering perennial prized for its colorful foliage.

Growing

Loosestrife grows well in **light shade** or **partial shade**. The soil should be of **average fertility, humus rich** and **moist**. Divide this plant in spring or fall. The trailing stems can be cut back if they begin to spread farther than you would like.

Tips

An attractive and care-free addition to the moist border, loosestrife is a good plant to include in a rock garden, along a rock wall or in a container where the trailing stems will have room to spread freely.

Recommended

L. nummularia is a prostrate, spreading plant with trailing stems. It bears bright yellow flowers in summer. A yellow-leaved cultivar, called **'Aurea,'** is popular and frequently available.

Also called: creeping Jenny **Features:** attractive foliage; summer flowers **Flower color:** yellow **Height:** 2–4" **Spread:** 18" or more **Hardiness:** zones 2–8

Lungwort
Pulmonaria

The wide array of lungworts have highly attractive foliage that ranges in color from apple green to silver-spotted and olive to dark emerald.

Growing

Lungworts prefer **partial to full shade**. The soil should be **fertile, humus rich, moist** and **well drained**. Rot can occur in very wet soil.

Divide in early summer, after flowering, or in autumn. Provide the newly planted divisions with a lot of water to help them re-establish.

Tips

Lungworts make useful and attractive groundcovers for shady borders, woodland gardens and pond and stream edges.

Recommended

P. longifolia (long-leaved lungwort) forms a dense clump of long, narrow, white-spotted, green leaves and bears clusters of blue flowers.

P. officinalis (common lungwort, spotted dog) forms a loose clump of evergreen foliage, spotted with white.

To keep lungworts tidy and to show off the fabulous foliage, deadhead the plants by shearing them back lightly after they flower.

D. saccharata (above & below)

The flowers open pink and mature to blue. Cultivars are available.

P. saccharata (Bethlehem sage) forms a compact clump of large, white-spotted, evergreen leaves and purple, red or white flowers. Many cultivars are available.

Features: decorative, mottled foliage; spring flowers **Flower color:** blue, red, pink, white **Height:** 8–24" **Spread:** 8–36" **Hardiness:** zones 3–8

Meadow Rue

Thalictrum

T. aquilegifolium (above & below)

M eadow rues are tall without being overbearing. Their fluffy flowers sway gracefully in the wind on wiry stems above fine foliage.

Growing

Meadow rues prefer **light or partial shade** but tolerate full sun with moist soil. The soil should be **humus rich, moist** and **well drained**. Meadow rues dislike being disturbed; plants may take a while to re-establish once they have been divided.

Tips

Meadow rues look beautiful when naturalized in an open woodland or meadow garden. When located in the middle or at the back of a border, they make a soft backdrop for bolder plants and flowers.

Meadow rues often do not emerge until quite late in spring. Mark where you plant them so that you do not inadvertently disturb the roots when cultivating their beds before they begin to grow.

Recommended

T. aquilegifolium (columbine meadow rue) forms an upright mound with pink or white plumes of flowers. Cultivars are available.

T. rochebruneanum 'Lavender Mist' (lavender mist meadow rue) forms a narrow, upright clump. The blooms are lavender purple and have numerous, distinctive, yellow stamens.

Taller meadow rues may need some support if they are in an exposed location where a good wind may topple them.

Features: summer flowers; light, airy habit; attractive foliage **Flower color:** pink, purple, yellow, white **Height:** 2–5' **Spread:** 1–3' **Hardiness:** zones 3–8

Narrow Leaf Blue Star

Amsonia

A. hubrichtii (above & below)

Perennials are not known for spectacular fall color, but narrow leaf blue star breaks the mold with its spectacular display of stunning, golden yellow, autumn hues.

Growing

Narrow leaf blue star grows well in **full sun, partial shade** or **light shade**. The soil should be of **average fertility, moist** and **well drained**. Plants are drought tolerant once established. Divide the plant in spring to propagate more plants.

Narrow leaf blue star is native to the southeastern United States.

Also called: willow leaf blue star **Features:** spring through summer flowers; habit; foliage **Flower color:** blue **Height:** 30–36" **Spread:** 24–36" **Hardiness:** zones 4–9

Tips

These pretty plants have a fine, billowy appearance. Plant in groups of three to five to achieve the most stunning results.

Recommended

A. hubrichtii forms a clump of arching stems and narrow, bright green leaves. Clusters of small, light blue, star-shaped flowers are produced from late spring to mid-summer. This is followed by stunning, golden yellow, fall color.

Peony

Paeonia

P. lactiflora cultivars (above & below)

From the simple, single flowers to the extravagant doubles, it's easy to become mesmerized with these voluptuous plants. Once the fleeting, but magnificent, flower display is done, the foliage remains stellar throughout the growing season.

Place wire tomato or peony cages around the plants in early spring to support the heavy flowers. The foliage will grow up and around the wires and hide the cage.

Growing

Peonies prefer **full sun** but tolerate some shade. The planting site should be well prepared before the plants are introduced. Peonies like **fertile, humus-rich, moist, well-drained** soil, to which a lot of compost has been added. Mulch peonies lightly with compost in spring. Too much fertilizer, particularly nitrogen, causes floppy growth and retards blooming. Deadhead to keep plants looking tidy.

Tips

These wonderful plants look great in a border combined with other early bloomers. They can be underplanted with bulbs and other plants that will die down by mid-summer; the emerging foliage of the peonies will hide the dying foliage of the spring plants. Avoid planting peonies under trees, where they will have to compete for moisture and nutrients.

Planting depth determines whether a peony will flower. Tubers planted too shallow or, more commonly, too deep will not flower. The buds or eyes on the tuber should be 1⅓–2" below the soil surface.

Recommended

There are hundreds of peonies available. Cultivars come in a wide range of colors, may have single or double flowers, and may or may not be fragrant. Visit your local garden center to see what is available.

Features: spring and early-summer flowers; attractive foliage **Flower color:** white, cream white, yellow, pink, red, purple **Height:** 24–32" **Spread:** 24–32" **Hardiness:** zones 2–8

Pinks

Dianthus

From tiny and delicate to large and robust, this genus contains a wide variety of plants, many with spice-scented flowers.

Growing

Pinks prefer **full sun** but tolerate some light shade. A **well-drained, neutral or alkaline** soil is required. The most important factor in the successful cultivation of pinks is drainage—they hate to stand in water. Rocky outcroppings are the native habitat of many species.

Tips

Pinks make excellent plants for rock gardens and rock walls, and for edging flower borders and walkways. They can also be used in cutting gardens and even as groundcovers. To prolong blooming, deadhead as the flowers fade, but leave a few flowers in place to go to seed.

Recommended

D. x *allwoodii* (allwood pinks) is a hybrid that forms a compact mound and bears flowers in a wide range of colors. Many cultivars are available.

D. *deltoides* (maiden pink) forms a mat of foliage and flowers in shades of red.

D. *gratianopolitanus* (cheddar pink) is long-lived and forms a very dense mat of evergreen, silver gray foliage with sweet-scented flowers, mostly in shades of pink.

D. deltoides (above), *D. plumarius* (below)

D. *plumarius* (cottage pink) is noteworthy for its role in the development of many popular cultivars known collectively as garden pinks. The flowers can be single, semi-double or fully double and are available in many colors.

Pinks self-seed quite easily. Seedlings may differ from the parent plants, often with new and interesting results.

Features: sometimes-fragrant spring or summer flowers; attractive foliage **Flower color:** pink, red, white, purple **Height:** 2–18" **Spread:** 6–24" **Hardiness:** zones 3–9

Purple Coneflower
Echinacea

E. purpurea 'Magnus' and 'White Swan' (above),
E. purpurea (below)

Purple coneflower is a visual delight, with its mauve petals offset by a spiky, orange center.

Growing
Purple coneflower grows well in **full sun** or **very light shade**. It tolerates any well-drained soil but prefers an **average to rich** soil. The thick taproots make this plant drought resist-ant, but it prefers to have regular water. Divide every four years or so in spring or autumn.

Deadhead early in the season to prolong flowering. Later you may wish to leave the flower-heads in place to self-seed to provide winter interest. Pinch plants back or thin out the stems in early summer to encourage bushy growth that will be less prone to mildew.

Tips
Use purple coneflowers in meadow gardens and informal borders, either in groups or as single specimens.

The dry flowerheads make an interesting feature in autumn and winter gardens.

Recommended
E. purpurea is an upright plant that is covered in prickly hairs. It bears purple flowers with orangy centers. Cultivars are available, including selections with white or pink flowers. Some new hybrids offer an expanded color range of orange or yellow flowers.

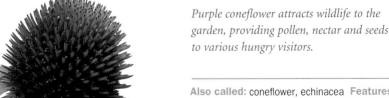

Purple coneflower attracts wildlife to the garden, providing pollen, nectar and seeds to various hungry visitors.

Also called: coneflower, echinacea **Features:** mid-summer to autumn flowers; persistent seedheads **Flower color:** purple, pink, yellow, orange, white; with rusty orange centers **Height:** 24–60" **Spread:** 12–24" **Hardiness:** zones 3–8

Russian Sage

Perovskia

P. atriplicifolia (above), *P. atriplicifolia* 'Filigran' (below)

Russian sage offers four-season interest in the garden: soft, gray-green leaves on light gray stems in spring; fuzzy, violet-blue flowers in summer; and silvery white stems in autumn that last until late winter.

Growing

Russian sage prefers **full sun**. The soil should be **poor to moderately fertile** and **well drained**. Too much water and nitrogen will cause this plant's growth to flop, so do not plant it next to heavy feeders. Russian sage cannot be divided because it is a subshrub that originates from a single stem.

Russian sage blossoms make a lovely addition to fresh bouquets and dried-flower arrangements.

In spring, when new growth appears low on the branches, or in autumn, cut the plant back hard to about 6–12" to encourage vigorous, bushy growth.

Tips

The silvery foliage and blue flowers soften the appearance of daylilies and work well with other plants in the back of a mixed border. Russian sage can also create a soft screen in a natural garden or on a dry bank.

Recommended

P. atriplicifolia is a loose, upright plant with silvery white, finely divided foliage. The small, lavender blue flowers are loosely held on silvery, branched stems. Cultivars are available.

Features: mid-summer to autumn flowers; attractive habit; fragrant, gray-green foliage **Flower color:** blue, purple **Height:** 3–4' **Spread:** 3–4' **Hardiness:** zones 4–9

Sedum

Sedum

S. 'Autumn Joy' (above & below)

Some 300 to 500 species of sedum are distributed throughout the Northern Hemisphere. Many sedums are grown for their foliage, which can range in color from steel gray-blue and green to red and burgundy.

Growing

Sedums prefer **full sun** but tolerate partial shade. The soil should be of average fertility, **very well drained** and **neutral to alkaline**. Divide in spring when needed.

Tips

Low-growing sedums make wonderful groundcovers and additions to rock gardens or rock walls. They also edge beds and borders beautifully. Taller sedums give a lovely late-season display in a bed or border.

Recommended

S. acre (gold moss stonecrop) is a low-growing, wide-spreading plant that bears small, yellow-green flowers.

S. '**Autumn Joy**' (autumn joy sedum) is a popular, upright hybrid. The flowers open pink or red and later fade to deep bronze.

S. spectabile (showy stonecrop) is an upright species with pink flowers. Cultivars are available.

S. spurium (two-row stonecrop) forms a low, wide mat of foliage with deep pink or white flowers. Many cultivars are available and are often grown for their colorful foliage.

Early-summer pruning of upright species and hybrids encourages compact, bushy growth but can delay flowering.

Also called: stonecrop **Features:** summer to autumn flowers; decorative, fleshy foliage **Flower color:** yellow, yellow-green, white, red, pink **Height:** 2–24" **Spread:** 12–24" or more **Hardiness:** zones 3–8

Toad Lily
Tricyrtis

T. hirta (above & below)

These plants, with their peculiar spotted flowers, are sure to draw attention to their shaded corner of the garden.

Growing

Toad lily grows well in **partial shade**, **light shade** or **full shade**. The soil should be **fertile, humus rich, moist** and **well drained**. Mulch in winter if snow cover is often inconsistent in your garden.

Tips

These diminutive plants are well suited to plantings in woodland gardens and shaded borders. If you have a shaded rock garden, patio or pond, these plants make good additions to locations where you can get up close to take a good look at the often-spotted flowers.

Recommended

T. hirta forms a clump of light green leaves. It bears white flowers, spotted with purple, in late summer and fall. Many wonderful cultivars are available.

If your toad lily fails to bloom before frost you may need to move it to a warmer location in the garden.

Also called: Japanese toad lily **Features:** late-summer and fall flowers; attractive foliage **Flower color:** white, blue, purple; with or without spots **Height:** 24–36" **Spread:** 12–24" **Hardiness:** zones 4–9

Aronia
Aronia

A. *melanocarpa* 'Autumn Magic' (above),
A. *melanocarpa* (below)

These lovely shrubs deserve to be more widely used in the garden. With clusters of white flowers in spring, glossy foliage that turns orange and red in fall, and decorative fruit that persists all winter, aronia has something to offer all year.

Growing

Aronia grows well in **full sun** or **partial shade,** with best flowering and fruiting in **full sun.** The soil should be of **average fertility** and **well drained,** though the plant adapts to most soil conditions. Wet, dry or poor soil conditions are tolerated.

Tips

Aronias are useful shrubs to include in shrub and mixed borders, and they make interesting, low-maintenance specimen plants. Left to their own devices they will colonize a fairly large area.

Recommended

A. arbutifolia (aronia, red chokeberry) is an upright shrub that bears white flowers in late spring, followed by bright red, waxy fruit in fall. The glossy, dark green foliage turns red in fall. Cultivars are available.

A. melanocarpa (aronia, black chokeberry) is an upright, suckering shrub native to Michigan and the eastern U.S. It bears white flowers in late spring, followed by black fruit in fall. The glossy, green foliage turns bright red to purple in fall. **'Viking'** and IROQUOIS BEAUTY are particularly attractive selections.

Aronia fruit is high in vitamins, especially vitamin C. The fruit was used as a source of vitamin C in Eastern Europe during the Cold War when citrus was often unavailable.

Also called: chokeberry **Features:** attractive, spring flowers; fall fruit; colorful, fall foliage **Habit:** suckering, deciduous shrub **Flower color:** white **Height:** 3–6' **Spread:** 3–10' **Hardiness:** zones 3–8

Barberry

Berberis

The variations available in plant size, foliage color and fruit make barberry a real workhorse of the plant world.

Growing

Barberry develops the best fall color when grown in **full sun,** but it tolerates partial shade. Any **well-drained** soil is suitable. This plant tolerates drought and urban conditions but suffers in poorly drained, wet soil.

Tips

Large barberry plants make great barrier or security hedges with formidable prickles. Barberry can also be included in shrub and mixed borders. Small cultivars can be grown in rock gardens, in raised beds and along rock walls.

Recommended

B. thunbergii (Japanese barberry) is a dense shrub with a broad, rounded habit. The foliage is bright green and turns variable shades of orange, red or purple in fall. Yellow spring flowers are followed by glossy, red fruit later in summer. Many cultivars have been developed for their variable foliage color, including shades of purple, yellow and variegated varieties. HELMOND PILLAR is an exceptionally narrow, upright selection and **'Concorde'** is a dwarf selection with deep purple foliage.

'Helmond Pillar' (above), 'Atropurpurea' (below)

Features: attractive foliage; flowers; fruit **Habit:** prickly, deciduous shrub **Flower color:** yellow **Height:** 1–6' **Spread:** 1½–6' **Hardiness:** zones 4–8

Beautyberry
Callicarpa

C. japonica (above), *C. dichotoma* 'Early Amethyst' (below)

This florists' favorite adds pizzazz to your fall garden. Even though these plants tend to die back during Michigan winters, they dependably produce a stunning display of pinkish purple fruit every fall.

Growing

Beautyberry grows well in **full sun** or **light shade**. The soil should be of **average fertility** and **well drained**. These shrubs often die back completely each winter, but fresh growth sprouts from the roots in spring, and flowers and fruit are produced on this new growth. Prune back dead branches in spring.

Tips

Beautyberries can be used in naturalistic gardens and in shrub and mixed borders, where the uniquely colored fruit will add interest and contrast.

The fruit-covered branches are often cut for fresh or dried arrangements as the colorful fruit persists on cut and dried branches.

Recommended

C. dichotoma (purple beautyberry) is a bushy, upright shrub with arching branches that are laden with dense clusters of purple fruit in fall. It grows 3–4' tall, with an equal or slightly greater spread. '**Early Amethyst**' and '**Issai**' are very good cultivars.

C. japonica (Japanese beautyberry) is a large, open shrub with arching branches and decorative, purple fruit in fall. It can grow up to 10' tall but usually only grows 4' when it is killed back each winter. The plant can spread 4–6'. A white-fruited cultivar called '**Leucocarpa**' is available.

Features: arching stems that bear late-summer or fall fruit **Habit:** bushy, deciduous shrub **Height:** 3–10' **Spread:** 3–6' **Hardiness:** zones 5–10

Beech

Fagus

The aristocrats of the large shade trees, the majestic beeches are certainly not the fastest growing trees, but they are among the most beautiful.

Growing

Beeches grow equally well in **full sun** or **partial shade**. The soil should be of **average fertility, loamy** and **well drained,** though almost all well-drained soils are tolerated.

American beech doesn't like having its roots disturbed and should be transplanted only when very young. European beech transplants easily and is more tolerant of varied soil conditions than is American beech.

Tips

Beeches make excellent specimens. They are also used as shade trees and in woodland gardens. These trees need a lot of space, but the European beech's adaptability to pruning makes it a reasonable choice in a small garden.

Recommended

F. grandifolia (American beech) is a broad-canopied tree, native to most of eastern North America.

F. sylvatica (European beech) is a spectacular broad tree with a number

F. grandiflora (above), *F. sylvatica* (below)

of interesting cultivars. Several are small enough to use in the home garden, from narrow columnar and weeping varieties to varieties with purple or yellow leaves, or pink, white and green variegated foliage.

Beech nuts are edible when roasted.

Features: attractive foliage; bark; habit; fall color; fruit **Habit:** large, oval, deciduous shade tree **Height:** 30–80' **Spread:** 10–65' **Hardiness:** zones 4–8

Birch

Betula

B. nigra (above & below)

When it comes to showy bark, the birch tree is unmatched. As it ages, its attractive, peeling bark adds a whole new dimension to the garden.

Growing

Birches grow well in **full sun, partial shade** or **light shade**. The soil should be of **average to high fertility, moist** and **fairly well drained**. Periodic flooding is tolerated but persistently wet soils will kill these trees.

Tips

Birch trees are often used as specimens. Their small leaves and open canopy provide light shade that allows perennials, annuals and lawns to flourish underneath. If you have enough space in your garden, birches look attractive when grown in groups near natural or artificial water features.

Recommended

B. lenta (cherry birch) has glossy, serrated leaves and brown-black bark. The fall color is a delicate gold. It grows 25–50' tall and spreads 20–45' wide.

B. nigra (river birch, black birch, red birch) has shaggy, cinnamon brown bark that flakes off in sheets when the tree is young, but the bark thickens and becomes more ridged as the tree matures. It grows 60–90' tall and spreads 40–60'. This species is resistant to pests and diseases. The cultivar **'Heritage'** is noted for its exceptional, peeling bark.

B. platyphylla var. ***japonica*** **'White-spire'** (Asian white birch) is an upright tree with striking, white bark that does not exfoliate. It grows about 40' tall and spreads 15–20'. This tree is extremely resistant to bronze birch borers. **'Crimson Frost'** is a purple-leaved cultivar of *B. platyphylla* var. *szechuanica* and *B. pendula* **'Purpurea.'**

The bark of B. papyrifera *(paper birch) has been used to make canoes, shelters, utensils and—as both the scientific and common names imply—paper.*

Features: attractive foliage; bark; fall color; winter and spring catkins **Habit:** open, deciduous tree **Height:** 25–90' **Spread:** 15–60' **Hardiness:** zones 3–8

Boxwood

Buxus

Boxwood's dense growth and small leaves form an even, green surface, which, along with its slow rate of growth, make this plant among the most popular for creating low hedges and topiaries.

Growing

Boxwoods prefer **partial shade** but adapt to full sun if kept well watered. The soil should be **fertile** and **well drained**. Once established, these plants are drought tolerant. A good, rich mulch benefits these shrubs because their roots grow very close to the surface. Try not to disturb the soil around established boxwoods because the roots are easily damaged.

B. microphylla var. *koreana* (above), *B. sempervirens* (below)

Tips

Boxwoods make excellent background plants in a mixed border. Brightly colored flowers show up well against the even, dark green surface of boxwoods. Dwarf cultivars can be trimmed into small hedges for edging garden beds or walkways. An interesting topiary piece can create a formal or whimsical focal point in any garden. Larger species and cultivars are often used to form dense, evergreen hedges.

Recommended

B. microphylla **var.** *koreana* (Korean boxwood) grows about 4' tall, with an equal spread. The bright green foliage may turn bronze, brown or yellow in winter. It is hardy to zone 4. Cultivars are available.

B. sempervirens (common boxwood) can grow up to 20' tall, with an equal spread if it is left unpruned. The foliage stays green all winter. This species requires a sheltered location as it is prone to winter damage. NORTH STAR is a good, hardy cultivar for Michigan.

Some of the best boxwood selections are cultivars developed from crosses between the two listed species. These hybrids combine the cold hardiness and pest resistance of Korean boxwood with the vigor and attractive winter color of common boxwood. CHICAGOLAND GREEN, 'Green Velvet' and 'Green Mountain' are all good, hardy selections well suited for Michigan.

Boxwood foliage contains toxic compounds that, when ingested, can cause severe digestive upset.

Features: attractive foliage **Habit:** dense, rounded, evergreen shrub **Height:** 2–20' **Spread:** 2–20' **Hardiness:** zones 4–8

Butterfly Bush
Buddleia

are drought tolerant once established. Plants flower on the current year's growth, so even if plants are killed back over the winter, they will still produce blooms.

Tips

Butterfly bushes make beautiful additions to shrub and mixed borders. Their graceful, arching habit makes them ideal as specimen plants. The dwarf forms that stay under 5' are suitable for small gardens.

Recommended

B. davidii (orange-eye butterfly bush, summer lilac) is the most commonly grown species. It grows 4–10' tall, with an equal spread. It bears fragrant flowers in bright and pastel shades of purple, pink, blue or white from midsummer through fall. The cultivars **'White Ball,' 'Pink Delight'** and **'Potters Purple'** are very good selections with large flowers and good branching. A number of semidwarf cultivars are sold under the **English Butterfly Series** name.

This attractive bush with its fragrant flowers will attract countless butterflies, along with a wide variety of other pollinating insects to your garden.

Growing

Butterfly bushes prefer to grow in **full sun;** they produce few, if any, flowers in shady conditions. The soil should be **fertile to average** and **well drained.** The plants

Butterfly bushes are among the best shrubs for attracting butterflies and bees to your garden, so avoid spraying your plant for pests—you will harm the beautiful and beneficial insects that make their homes there.

Features: attractive flowers; habit; foliage **Habit:** large, deciduous shrub with arching branches **Flower color:** purple, pink, blue, white **Height:** 4–12' **Spread:** 4–10' **Hardiness:** zones 5–9

Caryopteris
Caryopteris

Caryopteris is cultivated for its aromatic stems, foliage and flowers. A few cut stems in a vase will delicately scent a room.

Growing

Caryopteris prefers **full sun,** but it tolerates light shade. It does best in soil of **average fertility** that is **light** and **well drained**. Wet and poorly drained soils can kill this plant. Caryopteris is very drought tolerant once established. It can be treated as a herbaceous perennial if growth is regularly killed back over the winter.

Tips

Include caryopteris in your shrub or mixed border. The bright blue, late-season flowers are welcome when many other plants are past their flowering best.

Recommended

C. x *clandonensis* forms a dense mound up to 36" tall and 3–5' in spread. It bears clusters of blue, purple or pink flowers in late summer and early fall. 'First Choice' and PETIT BLEU are very good selections with compact branching, and 'Pink Chablis' is a new cultivar with loads of soft pink flowers.

C. x *clandonensis* 'Worrester Gold' (above),
C. x *clandonensis* (below)

C. incana is a larger, woodier shrub that grows to 4' tall and 3–5' in spread. It bears clusters of blue or purple flowers in late summer and early fall. SUNSHINE BLUE is a new selection with bright yellow foliage.

Caryopteris is sometimes killed back over cold winters. If you cut back the dead growth in spring, new shoots will sprout from the base, providing you with plenty of late-summer flowers.

Also called: bluebeard, blue spirea, blue mist **Features:** attractive, fragrant foliage; twigs; late-summer flowers **Habit:** rounded, spreading, deciduous shrub **Flower color:** pink, blue, purple **Height:** 2–4' **Spread:** 2–5' **Hardiness:** zones 5–9

Cedar
Thuja

T. occidentalis 'Yellow Ribbon' (above),
T. occidentalis (below)

Cedars are rot resistant, durable and long-lived, earning quiet admiration from gardeners everywhere.

Growing

Cedars prefer **full sun** but tolerate light to partial shade. The soil should be of **average fertility, moist** and **well drained**. These plants enjoy humidity, and in the wild they are often found growing near marshy areas. Cedars

will perform best in a location with some shelter from wind, especially in winter, when the foliage can easily dry out and give the entire plant a rather brown, drab appearance.

Tips

The large varieties of cedar make excellent specimen trees; smaller cultivars can be used in foundation plantings and shrub borders and as formal or informal hedges.

Recommended

T. occidentalis (eastern arborvitae, eastern white cedar) is a narrow, pyramidal tree with scale-like, evergreen needles. There are dozens of cultivars available, including shrubby dwarf varieties, varieties with yellow foliage and smaller, upright varieties. (Zones 2–7; some cultivars may be less cold hardy)

T. plicata (western arborvitae, western red cedar) is a narrowly pyramidal evergreen tree that grows quickly, resists deer browsing and maintains good foliage color all winter. Several cultivars are available, including several dwarf varieties and a yellow and green variegated variety. **'Green Giant,'** SPRING GROVE and **'Zebrina'** are good, hardy cultivars recommended for Michigan. (Zones 5–9)

Deer enjoy eating the foliage of eastern arborvitae. Consider using western arborvitae instead, which is relatively resistant to deer browsing.

Also called: arborvitae **Features:** attractive foliage; bark; form **Habit:** small to large, evergreen shrub or tree **Height:** 2–50' **Spread:** 2–20' **Hardiness:** zones 2–8

Cotoneaster
Cotoneaster

C. apiculatus (above), *C. dammeri* (below)

With their diverse sizes, shapes, flowers, fruit and foliage, cotoneasters are so versatile that if they weren't so lovely they would border on being overused.

Growing

Cotoneasters grow well in **full sun** or **partial shade**. The soil should be of **average fertility** and **well drained**.

Tips

Cotoneasters can be included in shrub or mixed borders. Low spreaders work well as groundcover, and shrubby species can be used to form hedges. Larger species are grown as small specimen trees; some low growers are grafted onto standards and grown as small, weeping trees.

Recommended

There are many cotoneasters to choose from. *C. adpressus* (creeping cotoneaster), *C.* x **'Hessei'** and *C. horizontalis* (rockspray cotoneaster) are low-growing, groundcover plants. *C. apiculatus* (cranberry cotoneaster) and *C. dammeri* (bearberry cotoneaster) are wide-spreading, low, shrubby plants. *C. salicifolius* (willowleaf cotoneaster) is an upright, shrubby plant that can be trained to form a small tree. These are just a few possibilities; your local garden center can help you find a suitable one for your garden.

Features: attractive foliage; early-summer flowers; persistent fruit; variety of forms **Habit:** evergreen or deciduous groundcover, shrub or small tree **Flower color:** white to pink **Height:** 6"–15' **Spread:** 3–12' **Hardiness:** zones 4–8

Crabapple

Malus

M. 'Royalty' (above)

Loads of spring flowers, a brilliant display of colorful autumn fruit and exceptional winter hardiness—what more could anyone ask from a small, flowering tree?

Growing

Crabapples prefer **full sun** but tolerate partial shade. The soil should be of **average to rich fertility, moist** and **well drained**. These trees tolerate damp soil but will suffer in wet locations.

Tips

Crabapples make excellent specimen plants. Many varieties are quite small, so there is one to suit almost any size of garden. Some forms are even small enough to grow in large containers. Crabapples' flexible, young branches make these trees good choices for creating espalier specimens along a wall or fence.

Recommended

There are hundreds of crabapples available. When choosing a species, variety or cultivar, one of the most important attributes to look for is disease resistance. Even the most beautiful flowers, fruit or habit will never look good if the plant is ravaged by pests or diseases. Ask for information about new, resistant cultivars at your local nursery or garden center.

Features: attractive, spring flowers; late-season and winter fruit; fall foliage; habit; bark **Habit:** rounded, mounded or spreading, small to medium, deciduous tree **Flower color:** white, pink, red, purple-red **Height:** 5–30' **Spread:** 6–30' **Hardiness:** zones 4–8

Dogwood

Cornus

W hether your garden is wet, dry, sunny or shaded, there is a dogwood for almost every condition. Stem color, leaf variegation, fall color, growth habit, soil adaptability and hardiness are all positive attributes to be found in the dogwoods.

Growing

Dogwoods grow equally well in **full sun, light shade** or **partial shade**, with a slight preference for light shade. The soil should be of **average to high fertility, high in organic matter, neutral or slightly acidic** and **well drained**.

Tips

Shrub dogwoods can be included in a shrub or mixed border. They look best in groups rather than as single specimens. The tree species make wonderful specimen plants and are small enough to include in most gardens. Use them along the edge of a woodland, in a shrub or mixed border, alongside a house, or near a pond, water feature or patio.

Recommended

C. alba (red-twig dogwood, Tartarian dogwood) and *C. sericea* (*C. stolonifera*; red-osier dogwood) species and cultivars are grown for their bright red stems that provide winter interest. Cultivars are available with stems in varied shades of red, orange and yellow. Fall foliage color can also be attractive. (Zones 2–8)

C. alba 'Bailhalo' IVORY HALO (above),
C. kousa var. *chinensis* (below)

C. alternifolia (pagoda dogwood) can be grown as a large, multi-stemmed shrub or a small, single-stemmed tree. The branches have an attractive, layered appearance. Clusters of small, white flowers appear in early summer. The cultivar **'Argentia'** has silver and green variegated leaves, and a new selection, GOLDEN SHADOWS, has large, golden variegated leaves. (Zones 3–8)

C. kousa (Kousa dogwood) is grown for its flowers, fruit, fall color and interesting bark. The white-bracted flowers are followed by bright red fruit. The foliage turns red and purple in fall. **Var. chinensis** (Chinese dogwood) grows more vigorously and has larger flowers. The cultivar **'Satomi'** has soft, pink flowers. (Zones 5–9)

Features: late-spring to early-summer flowers; fall foliage; stem color; fruit
Habit: deciduous, large shrub or small tree **Flower color:** white **Height:** 5–30'
Spread: 5–30' **Hardiness:** zones 2–9

Elder

Sambucus

S. racemosa (above & below)

Elders work well in a naturalized garden. Cultivars are available that will provide light texture in a dark area, dark foliage in a bright area, or variegated yellow foliage and bright stems in brilliant sunshine.

Growing

Elders grow well in **full sun** or **partial shade**. Cultivars and varieties grown for interesting leaf color develop the best color in light or partial shade. The soil should be of **average fertility, moist** and **well drained**. These plants tolerate dry soil once they are established.

Tips

Elders can be used in a shrub or mixed border, in a natural woodland garden, or next to a pond or other water feature. Types with interesting or colorful foliage can be used as specimen plants or focal points in the garden.

Recommended

S. canadensis (American elder/elderberry), *S. nigra* (European elder/elderberry, black elder/elderberry) and *S. racemosa* (European red elder/elderberry) are rounded shrubs with white or pinkish white flowers followed by red or dark purple berries. Cultivars are available with green, yellow, bronze or purple foliage and deeply divided, feathery foliage. BLACK BEAUTY, BLACK LACE, 'Madonna' and 'Sutherland' are all exceptional cultivars for Michigan.

Also called: elderberry **Features:** early-summer flowers; fruit; foliage **Habit:** large, bushy, deciduous shrub **Flower color:** white, pinkish white **Height:** 5–20' **Spread:** 5–20' **Hardiness:** zones 3–9

Euonymus
Euonymus

Euonymus works well as a background or border plant for its stunning fall color and interesting bark, and it also makes a fine specimen as a small tree. The evergreen wintercreeper euonymus, with its interesting leaf colorings and plant habits, also has many uses.

Growing
Euonymus species prefer **full sun** but tolerate light or partial shade. Soil of **average to rich fertility** is preferable but any **moist, well-drained** soil will do.

Tips
E. alatus can be grown in a shrub or mixed border, as a specimen, in a naturalistic garden or as a hedge. Dwarf cultivars can be used to create informal hedges. *E. fortunei* can be grown as a shrub in borders or as a hedge. It is an excellent substitute for the more demanding boxwood. The trailing habit also makes it useful as a groundcover or climber.

Recommended
E. alatus (burning bush, winged euonymus) is an attractive, open, mounding, deciduous shrub with vivid, red fall foliage. Winter interest is provided by the corky ridges, or

E. alatus 'Cole's Select' (above),
E. fortunei cultivar (below)

wings, that grow on the stems and branches. The cultivars **'Compacta'** and FIRE BALL are noted for their excellent fall color; **'Rudy Haag'** is a dwarf selection that produces little to no fruit.

E. fortunei (wintercreeper euonymus) is rarely grown as a species owing to the wide and attractive variety of cultivars. These can be prostrate, climbing or mounding evergreens, often with attractive, variegated foliage. **'Emerald Gaiety'** and BLONDY are cultivars noted for their colorful, variegated foliage.

E. alatus achieves the best fall color when grown in full sun.

Features: attractive foliage; corky stems (*E. alatus*) **Habit:** deciduous or evergreen shrub, small tree, groundcover or climber **Height:** 1½–20' **Spread:** 1½–20' **Hardiness:** zones 3–9

False Cypress
Chamaecyparis

C. pisifera threadleaf cultivar (above), *C. nootkatensis* 'Pendula' (below)

Conifer shoppers are blessed with a marvelous selection of false cypresses that offer color, size, shape and growth habits not available in most other evergreens.

Growing
False cypresses prefer **full sun to partial shade**. The soil should be **fertile, moist, neutral to acidic** and **well drained**. Alkaline soils are tolerated. In shaded areas, growth may be sparse or thin.

The oils in the foliage of false cypresses may irritate sensitive skin.

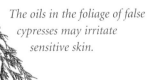

Tips
Tree varieties are used as specimen plants and for hedging. The dwarf and slow-growing cultivars are used in borders and rock gardens and as bonsai. False cypress shrubs can be grown near the house or as evergreen specimens in large containers.

Recommended
There are several available species of false cypress and many cultivars. The scaly foliage can be in a drooping or strand-like form, in fan-like or feathery sprays and may be dark green, bright green or yellow. Plant forms vary too, from mounding or rounded, to tall and pyramidal, or narrow with pendulous branches. Check with your local garden center or nursery to see what is available.

Features: attractive foliage; habit; cones **Habit:** narrow, pyramidal, evergreen tree or shrub **Height:** 1½–150' **Spread:** 1½–80' **Hardiness:** zones 4–8

Flowering Cherry, Plum & Almond

Prunis

Cherries are so beautiful and uplifting after the gray days of winter that few gardeners can resist them.

Growing

These flowering fruit trees prefer **full sun**. The soil should be of **average fertility, moist** and **well drained**. Shallow roots will emerge from the lawn if the tree is not getting sufficient water.

Tips

Prunus species are beautiful as specimen plants and many are small enough to be included in almost any garden. Smaller species and cultivars can also be included in borders or grouped to form informal hedges or barriers. Pissard plum and purpleleaf sand cherry can be trained to form formal hedges.

Because of the pest problems that afflict many of the cherries, they can be rather short-lived. Choose resistant species such as Sargent cherry or Higan cherry. If you plant a more susceptible species, such as the Japanese flowering cherry, enjoy it while it thrives but be prepared to replace it.

Recommended

Following are a few popular selections from the many species, hybrids and cultivars available. Check with your local nursery or garden center for other possible selections. *P. cerasifera*

P. subhirtella 'Pendula Rosea' (above)

'**Atropurpurea**' (Pissard plum) and *P.* x *cistena* (purpleleaf sand cherry) are shrubby plants grown for their purple foliage and light pink flowers. *P. sargentii* (Sargent cherry), *P. serrulata* (Japanese flowering cherry) and *P. subhirtella* (Higan cherry) are rounded or spreading trees grown for their white or light pink flowers as well as for their often-attractive bark and bright fall color.

The fruits, but not the pits, of Prunus *species are edible but not very tasty. Eating too much of the often-sour fruit can cause stomach aches.*

Features: attractive, spring to early-summer flowers; fruit; bark; fall foliage
Habit: upright, rounded, spreading or weeping deciduous tree or shrub
Flower color: pink, white **Height:** 4–75'
Spread: 4–50' **Hardiness:** zones 3–9

Forsythia
Forsythia

F. x *intermedia* (above & below)

These shrubs are treated a bit like relatives. It's fabulous to see them when they burst into bloom after a long, dreary winter, but they just seem to be taking up garden space once they are done flowering. The introduction of new selections with more decorative foliage has made them more appealing.

Growing

Forsythias grow best in **full sun,** but some selections tolerate or prefer **light or partial shade.** The soil should be of **average fertility, moist** and **well drained.** These plants are more cold hardy than their flower buds. In a sheltered spot, or if covered by snow for the winter, forsythias may flower in a colder than recommended hardiness zone.

Tips

These shrubs are gorgeous while in flower but most aren't very interesting for the rest of the year. Include forsythias in a shrub or mixed border where other flowering plants will provide interest once the forsythias' early-season glory has passed.

Recommended

F. x *intermedia* is a large shrub with upright stems that arch as they mature. It grows 5–10' tall and spreads 5–12'. Bright yellow flowers emerge in early to mid-spring, before the leaves. Many cultivars are available. A few of the better selections include GOLDEN PEEP, GOLD TIDE, 'New Hampshire Gold' and the variegated selections 'Kumson' and 'Fiesta.'

Forsythias can be used as hedging plants, but they look most attractive and flower best when grown informally.

Features: attractive, early to mid-spring flowers **Habit:** spreading, deciduous shrub with upright or arching branches **Flower color:** yellow **Height:** 2–10' **Spread:** 3–15' **Hardiness:** zones 5–8

Fothergilla
Fothergilla

*F*lowers, fragrance, fall color and interesting, soft tan to brownish stems give fothergillas year-round appeal.

Growing

Fothergilla grows equally well in **full sun** or **partial shade**, but these plants will bear the most flowers and have the best fall color in full sun. The soil should be of **average fertility, acidic, humus rich, moist** and **well drained**.

Tips

Fothergilla is attractive and useful in shrub or mixed borders, in woodland gardens and when combined with evergreen groundcover.

F. gardenii 'Blue Mist' (above), *F. major* (below)

Recommended

Cultivars are available for both species.

F. gardenii (dwarf fothergilla) is a bushy shrub that bears fragrant, white flowers. The foliage turns yellow, orange and red in fall.

F. major (large fothergilla) is a larger, rounded shrub that bears fragrant, white flowers. The autumn colors are yellow, orange and scarlet. **'Blue Shadow'** is an exceptional, new cultivar with attractive, blue foliage.

The bottlebrush-shaped flowers of fothergilla have a delicate, honey scent. The shrubs are generally problem free and make wonderful companions to azaleas, rhododendrons and other acid-loving, woodland plants.

Features: fragrant, spring flowers; fall foliage **Habit:** dense, rounded or bushy, deciduous shrub **Flower color:** white **Height:** 2–10' **Spread:** 2–10' **Hardiness:** zones 4–9

Fringe Tree
Chionanthus

C. virginicus (above & below)

Growing

Fringe trees prefer **full sun**. They do best in soil that is **fertile, acidic, moist** and **well drained** but will adapt to most soil conditions. In the wild they are often found growing alongside stream banks.

Tips

Fringe trees work well as specimen plants, as part of a border or beside a water feature. These plants begin flowering at a very early age.

Recommended

C. retusus (Chinese fringe tree) is a rounded, spreading shrub or small tree with deeply furrowed, peeling bark and erect, fragrant, white flower clusters. (Zones 5–9)

Fringe trees adapt to a wide range of growing conditions. They are cold hardy and are densely covered in silky, white, honey-scented flowers that shimmer in the wind over a long period in spring.

C. virginicus (white fringe tree) is a spreading, small tree or large shrub that bears drooping, fragrant, white flowers.

Fringe trees can be very difficult to find in general nurseries. Specialty nurseries, mail-order nurseries and plant sales at botanical gardens are the most likely places to find them. They are well worth hunting for.

Features: fragrant, early-summer flowers; bark **Habit:** rounded or spreading, deciduous, large shrub or small tree **Flower color:** white **Height:** 10–25' **Spread:** 10–25' **Hardiness:** zones 4–9

Golden Rain Tree
Koelreutaria

K. paniculata (above & below)

With its delicate clusters of yellow flowers and overall lacy appearance in summer, this lovely tree deserves wider use as a specimen or shade tree.

Growing
Golden rain tree grows best in **full sun**. The soil should be **average to fertile, moist** and **well drained**. This tree tolerates heat, drought, wind and air pollution. It also adapts to most pH levels and is fast growing.

Tips
Golden rain tree makes an excellent shade or specimen tree for small properties. Its ability to adapt to a wide range of soils makes it useful in many garden situations. The fruit is not messy and will not stain a patio or deck if planted to shade these areas.

Recommended
K. paniculata is an attractive, rounded, spreading tree. It bears long clusters of small, yellow flowers in mid-summer, followed by red-tinged, green capsular fruit. The leaves are attractive and somewhat lacy in appearance. The foliage may turn bright yellow in fall. Cultivars are available.

This Asian species is one of the few trees with yellow flowers and one of the only trees to bloom in mid- or late summer.

Features: attractive foliage; fruit; mid- or late-summer flowers **Habit:** rounded, spreading, deciduous tree **Flower color:** yellow **Height:** 30–40' **Spread:** 30–40' **Hardiness:** zones 5–8

Hawthorn

Crataegus

C. *phaenopyrum* (above),
C. *laevigata* 'Paul's Scarlet' (below)

The hawthorns are uncommonly beautiful trees, with a generous spring show of beautiful, apple-like blossoms, persistent, glossy, red fruit and often good fall color.

Growing

Hawthorns grow equally well in **full sun** or **partial shade**. They adapt to any **well-drained** soil and tolerate urban conditions.

Tips

Hawthorns can be grown as specimen plants or hedges in urban sites, lakeside gardens and exposed locations. They are popular in areas where vandalism is a problem because very few people wish to grapple with plants bearing stiff, 2" long thorns. As a hedge, hawthorns create an almost impenetrable barrier.

These trees are small enough to include in most gardens. With their long, sharp thorns, however, hawthorns might not be a good selection if there are children about.

Recommended

C. laevigata (*C. oxycantha*; English hawthorn) is a low-branching, rounded tree with zigzag layers of thorny branches. It bears white or pink flowers, followed by red fruit in late summer. Many cultivars are available.

C. phaenopyrum (*C. cordata*; Washington hawthorn) is an oval to rounded, thorny tree that bears white flowers and persistent, shiny, red fruit in fall. The glossy green foliage turns red and orange in fall.

C. viridis 'Winter King' (Winter King hawthorn) is a medium-sized tree with a wide, oval habit. It is prized for its show of white, spring flowers, silver bark and brilliant display of large, red fruit that persists through winter.

Features: late-spring or early-summer flowers; fruit; foliage; thorny branches; habit **Habit:** rounded, deciduous tree, often with a zigzagged, layered branch pattern **Flower color:** white, pink **Height:** 15–35' **Spread:** 12–35' **Hardiness:** zones 3–8

Hemlock
Tsuga

T. canadensis 'Jeddeloh' (above), *T. canadensis* (below)

Many people would agree that eastern hemlock is one of the most beautiful, graceful evergreen trees in the world. The movement, softness and agility of this tree make it easy to place in the landscape.

Growing

Hemlock generally grows well in any light from **full sun to full shade**. The soil should be **humus rich, moist** and **well drained**. Hemlock is drought sensitive and grows best in cool, moist conditions. It is also sensitive to air pollution and suffers salt damage, so keep hemlock away from roadways.

With the continued popularity of water gardening, hemlock is in demand for the naturalizing effect it has on pondscapes.

Tips

This elegant tree, with its delicate needles, is one of the most beautiful evergreens to use as a specimen tree. Hemlock can also be trimmed to form a hedge. The smaller cultivars may be included in a shrub or mixed border. Hemlock can be pruned to keep it within bounds or shaped to form a hedge. The many dwarf forms are useful in smaller gardens.

Recommended

T. canadensis (eastern hemlock, Canadian hemlock) is a graceful, narrowly pyramidal tree. Many cultivars are available, including groundcover and pendulous and dwarf forms.

Features: attractive foliage; cones **Habit:** pyramidal or columnar, evergreen tree or shrub **Height:** 1½–80' **Spread:** 1½–35' **Hardiness:** zones 3–8

Holly
Ilex

I. x meserveae cultivar (above),
I. x meserveae 'Blue Girl' (below)

Hollies vary greatly in shape and size and can be such delights when placed with full consideration for their needs.

Growing

These plants prefer **full sun** but tolerate partial shade. The soil should be of **average to rich fertility, humus rich** and **moist**. Hollies perform best in acidic soil with a pH of 6.5 or lower. Shelter hollies from winter wind to help prevent the evergreen leaves from drying out. Apply a summer mulch to keep the roots cool and moist.

Tips

Hollies can be used in groups, in woodland gardens and in shrub and mixed borders. They can also be shaped into hedges. Winterberry is good for naturalizing in moist sites in the garden.

Recommended

I. glabra (inkberry) is a rounded shrub with glossy, deep green, evergreen foliage and dark purple fruit. Some of the better cultivars include **'Shamrock,' 'Nigra'** and **'Compacta.'** (Zones 4–9)

I. x meserveae (meserve holly, blue holly) is a group of hybrids that originated from crosses between tender English holly (*I. aquifolium*) and hardy hollies like prostrate holly (*I. rugosa*). These dense, evergreen shrubs may be erect, mounding or spreading. Preferred cultivars include **'Blue Prince,' 'Blue Princess,'** CASTLE WALL and CASTLE SPIRE. (Zones 5–8)

I. verticillata (winterberry, winterberry holly) is a deciduous, native species grown for its explosion of red, orange or yellow fruit that persists into winter. Many cultivars and hybrids are available.

All hollies have male and female flowers on separate plants, and both must be present for the females to set fruit. One male plant will adequately pollinate two or three females.

Also called: inkberry, winterberry **Features:** attractive, glossy, sometimes spiny foliage; fruit; habit **Habit:** erect or spreading, evergreen or deciduous shrub or tree **Height:** 3–50' **Spread:** 3–40' **Hardiness:** zones 3–9

Hydrangea
Hydrangea

Hydrangeas have many attractive qualities including showy, often long-lasting flowers and glossy green leaves, some of which turn beautiful colors in fall.

Growing

Hydrangeas grow well in **full sun** or **partial shade,** and some species tolerate full shade. Shade or partial shade will reduce leaf and flower scorch in hotter gardens. The soil should be of **average to high fertility, humus rich, moist** and **well drained**. These plants perform best in cool, moist conditions.

Tips

Hydrangeas come in many forms and have many uses in the landscape. They can be included in shrub or mixed borders, used as specimens or informal barriers and planted in groups or containers.

Recommended

H. arborescens (smooth hydrangea) is a rounded shrub that flowers well, even in shady conditions. Superior selections include **'Annabelle'** and WHITE DOME.

H. paniculata (panicle hydrangea) is a spreading to upright, large shrub or small tree that bears white flowers from late summer to early fall. **'Grandiflora'** (Peegee hydrangea) is a commonly available cultivar. Other excellent selections include LIMELIGHT, **'Little Lamb'** and **'Pink Diamond.'**

H. arborescens 'Annabelle' (above), *H. paniculata* 'Grandiflora' (below)

H. quercifolia (oakleaf hydrangea) is a mound-forming shrub with attractive, cinnamon brown, exfoliating bark, large leaves that are lobed like an oak's and that turn bronze to bright red in fall and conical clusters of sterile and fertile flowers. Some of the lovely cultivars include **'Little Honey,' 'Pee Wee,' 'Snowflake'** and **'Snow Queen.'**

Features: attractive flowers, foliage and bark **Habit:** deciduous, mounding or spreading shrub or tree **Flower color:** white **Height:** 3–80' **Spread:** 3–20' **Hardiness:** zones 4–9

Juniper
Juniperus

J. squamata (above),
J. horizontalis 'Blue Prince' (below)

Tips

With the wide variety of junipers available, there are endless uses for them in the garden. They make prickly barriers and hedges, and they can be used in borders, as specimens or in groups. The larger species can be used to form windbreaks, while the low-growing species can be used in rock gardens and as groundcover.

Recommended

Junipers vary, not just from species to species, but often within a species. Cultivars are available for all species and may differ significantly from the species. ***J. chinensis*** (Chinese juniper) is a conical tree or spreading shrub. ***J. horizontalis*** (creeping juniper) is a prostrate, creeping groundcover. ***J. procumbens*** (Japanese garden juniper) is a wide-spreading, stiff-branched, low shrub. ***J. scopulorum*** (Rocky Mountain juniper) can be upright, rounded, weeping or spreading. ***J. squamata*** (singleseed juniper) forms a prostrate or low, spreading shrub or a small, upright tree. ***J. virginiana*** (eastern redcedar) is a durable, upright or wide-spreading tree.

There may be a juniper in every gardener's future, with all the choices available, from low creeping plants to upright pyramidal forms.

Growing

Junipers prefer **full sun** but tolerate light shade. Ideally, the soil should be of **average fertility** and **well drained,** but these plants tolerate most conditions.

It is a good idea to wear long sleeves and gloves when handling junipers as the prickly foliage gives some gardeners a rash. Juniper 'berries' are poisonous if eaten in large quantities.

Features: evergreen **Habit:** conical or columnar tree; rounded or spreading shrub; prostrate groundcover **Height:** 4"–80' **Spread:** 1½–25' **Hardiness:** zones 3–9

Katsura-Tree

Cercidiphyllum

The Katsura-tree is a classic tree that will add distinction and grace to the garden. Even in youth it is poised and elegant, and it is bound to become a bewitching, mature specimen.

Growing

Katsura-tree grows equally well in **full sun** or **partial shade**. The soil should be **fertile, humus rich, neutral to acidic, moist** and **well drained**. This tree will establish more quickly if watered regularly during dry spells for the first year or two.

Tips

Katsura-tree is useful as a specimen or shade tree. The species is quite large and is best used in large gardens. The cultivar **'Pendula'** is quite wide spreading but can be used in smaller gardens.

Recommended

C. japonicum is a slow-growing tree with heart-shaped, blue-green foliage that turns yellow and orange in fall and develops a spicy scent. The cultivar **'Pendula'** is one of the most elegant weeping trees available. It is usually grafted to a standard and the mounding, cascading branches give the entire tree the appearance of a waterfall tumbling over rocks.

C. japonicum 'Pendula' (above), *C. japonicum* (below)

This tree is native to eastern Asia, and the delicate foliage blends well into Japanese-style gardens.

Features: attractive summer and fall foliage
Habit: rounded, spreading or weeping, often multi-stemmed, deciduous tree **Height:** 10–65'
Spread: 10–65' **Hardiness:** zones 4–8

Lilac
Syringa

S. *meyeri* TINKERBELLE (above), S. *vulgans* (below)

The hardest thing about growing lilacs is choosing from the many species and hundreds of cultivars available.

Growing
Lilacs grow best in **full sun**. The soil should be **fertile, humus rich** and **well drained**. These plants tolerate open, windy locations.

Tips
Include lilacs in a shrub or mixed border or use them to create an informal hedge. Japanese tree lilac can be used as a specimen tree.

Recommended
S. x *hyacinthiflora* (hyacinth-flowered lilac, early-flowering lilac) is a group of hardy, upright hybrids that become spreading as they mature. Clusters of fragrant flowers appear two weeks earlier than those of the French lilacs. The leaves turn reddish purple in fall. Many excellent, disease-resistant cultivars are available. (Zones 3–7)

S. *meyeri* 'Palibin' (Palibin lilac) is a compact, rounded shrub that bears fragrant, pink or lavender flowers. (Zones 3–7)

S. *patula* 'Miss Kim' is a dwarf, compact lilac with pale, purple flower buds that open lavender blue. It shows attractive, dark green foliage and vigorous growth. (Zones 3–7)

S. *reticulata* (Japanese tree lilac) is a rounded, large shrub or small tree that bears white flowers. 'Ivory Silk' has a more compact habit and produces more flowers than the species. (Zones 3–7)

S. *vulgaris* (French lilac, common lilac) is the plant most people think of when they think of lilacs. It is a suckering, spreading shrub with an irregular habit that bears fragrant, lilac-colored flowers. Hundreds of cultivars with a variety of flower colors are available.

Lilacs are frost-loving shrubs that won't flower at all in the warm, southern parts of the U.S.

Features: attractive, late-spring to mid-summer flowers **Habit:** rounded or suckering, deciduous shrub or small tree **Flower color:** lilac, white, purple, pink, lavender **Height:** 3–30' **Spread:** 3–25' **Hardiness:** zones 2–8

Linden
Tilia

Lindens are picturesque shade trees with a signature gum-drop shape and sweet-scented flowers that capture the essence of summer.

Growing

Lindens grow best in **full sun**. The soil should be **average to fertile, moist** and **well drained**. These trees adapt to most pH levels but prefer an alkaline soil. They tolerate pollution and urban conditions.

Tips

Lindens are useful and attractive street trees, shade trees and specimen trees. Their tolerance of pollution and their moderate size make lindens ideal for city gardens.

Recommended

T. cordata (littleleaf linden) is a dense, pyramidal tree that may become rounded with age. It bears small, fragrant flowers with narrow, yellow-green bracts. Cultivars are available.

T. tomentosa (silver linden) has a broad, pyramidal or rounded habit that bears small, fragrant flowers and has glossy, green leaves with fuzzy, silvery undersides.

T. cordata (above)

Linden flowers are used to make a herbal tea.

Features: foliage; fragrant flowers
Habit: dense, pyramidal to rounded, deciduous tree **Flower color:** creamy white to pale yellow **Height:** 20–65'
Spread: 15–50' **Hardiness:** zones 3–8

Maple
Acer

A. ginnala 'Bailey Compact (above),
A. palmatum var. *dissectum* cultivar (below)

Growing

Generally, maples do well in **full sun** or **light shade,** though this varies from species to species. The soil should be **fertile, moist, high in organic matter** and **well drained.**

Tips

Maples can be used as specimen trees, as large elements in shrub or mixed borders or as hedges. Some are useful as understory plants bordering wooded areas; others can be grown in containers on patios or terraces. Few Japanese gardens are without the attractive smaller maples. Almost all maples can be used to create bonsai specimens.

Recommended

Maples are some of the most popular trees used as shade or street trees. Many are very large when fully mature, but there are also a few smaller species that are useful in smaller gardens, including **A. campestre** (hedge maple), **A. ginnala** (amur maple), **A. palmatum** (Japanese maple) and **A. rubrum** (red maple). Check with your local nursery or garden center for availability.

Maples are attractive all year, with delicate flowers in spring, attractive foliage and hanging samaras in summer, vibrant leaf color in fall and interesting bark and branch structures in winter.

Features: foliage; bark; winged fruit; fall color; form; flowers **Habit:** small, multi-stemmed, deciduous tree or large shrub **Flower color: Height:** 6–80' **Spread:** 6–70' **Hardiness:** zones 2–8

Ninebark

Physocarpus

P. opulifolius 'Dart's Gold' (above), *P. opulifolius* DIABLO (below)

This attractive native deserves wider recognition, especially now that attractive cultivars, with foliage ranging in color from yellow to purple, are available.

Growing

Ninebark grows well in **full sun** or **partial shade**. The best leaf coloring develops in a sunny location. The soil should be **fertile, acidic, moist** and **well drained**.

Tips

Ninebark can be included in a shrub or mixed border, in a woodland garden or in a naturalistic garden.

Recommended

P. opulifolius (common ninebark) is a suckering shrub with long, arching branches and exfoliating bark. It bears light pink flowers in early summer and fruit that ripens to reddish green in fall. Recommended cultivars include **'Dart's Gold'** and SUMMER WINE.

You may not actually find nine layers, but the peeling, flecked bark of ninebark does add interest to the winter landscape.

Also called: common ninebark **Features:** early-summer flowers; fruit; bark; foliage **Habit:** upright, sometimes suckering, deciduous shrub **Flower color:** pink **Height:** 4–10' **Spread:** 4–15' **Hardiness:** zones 2–8

Oak

Quercus

Q. robur (above & below)

The oak's classic shape, outstanding fall color, deep roots and long life are some of its many assets. Plant it for its individual beauty and for posterity.

Growing
Oaks grow well in **full sun** or **partial shade**. The soil should be **fertile, moist** and **well drained**. These trees can be difficult to establish; transplant them only when they are young.

Tips
Oaks are large trees that are best as specimens or for groves in parks and large gardens. Do not disturb the ground around the base of an oak; this tree is very sensitive to changes in grade.

A spring application of fertilizer will encourage vigorous, new growth on plants that have suffered winter dieback.

Recommended
There are many oaks to choose from. A few popular species are **Q. alba** (white oak), a rounded, spreading tree with peeling bark and purple-red fall color; **Q. coccinea** (scarlet oak), noted for having the most brilliant, red fall color of all the oaks; **Q. robur** (English oak), a rounded, spreading tree with golden yellow fall color; and **Q. rubra** (red oak) a rounded, spreading tree with fall color ranging from yellow to red-brown. Some cultivars are available; check with your local nursery or garden center.

Acorns are generally not edible, though acorns of certain oak species are edible but usually must be processed first to leach out the bitter tannins.

Features: summer and fall foliage; bark; acorns **Habit:** large, rounded, spreading, deciduous tree **Height:** 35–120'
Spread: 10–100' **Hardiness:** zones 3–9

Pine

Pinus

P. mugo (above), P. strobus (below)

Pines offer exciting possibilities for any garden. Exotic-looking pines are available with soft or stiff needles, needles with yellow bands, trunks with patterned or mother-of-pearl-like bark and varied forms.

Growing
Pines grow best in **full sun**. These trees adapt to most **well-drained** soils but do not tolerate polluted urban conditions.

Tips
Pines can be used as specimen trees, as hedges or to create windbreaks. Smaller cultivars can be included in shrub or mixed borders. These trees are not heavy feeders; fertilizing will encourage rapid new growth that is weak and susceptible to pest and disease problems.

Recommended
There are many available pines, both trees and shrubby dwarf plants. Check with your local garden center or nursery to find out what is available.

P. nigra (Austrian pine) was often recommended as the most urban-tolerant pine, but overplanting has led to severe disease problems, some of which can kill a tree in a single growing season.

Features: foliage; bark; cones **Habit:** upright, columnar or spreading, evergreen tree **Height:** 2–120' **Spread:** 2–60' **Hardiness:** zones 2–8

Potentilla

Potentilla

Too much fertilizer or too rich a soil will encourage weak, floppy, disease-prone growth.

Tips

Potentilla is useful in a shrub or mixed border. The smaller cultivars can be included in rock gardens and on rock walls. On slopes that are steep or awkward to mow, potentilla can prevent soil erosion and reduce the time spent maintaining the lawn. Potentilla can even be used to form a low, informal hedge.

Potentilla is a fuss-free shrub that blooms madly all summer. The cheery, yellow-flowered variety is often seen, but there are also cultivars with flowers in shades of pink, red, orange or white.

Growing

Potentilla prefers **full sun** but tolerates partial or light shade. The soil should preferably be of **poor to average fertility** and **well drained**. This plant tolerates most conditions, including sandy or clay soil and wet or dry conditions. Established plants are drought tolerant.

Orange, red or pink potentilla flower colors may fade in hot weather or direct sunlight. The colors should revive in fall as the weather cools but try moving the plant to a cooler, more sheltered location.

Recommended

Of the many cultivars of **P. fruticosa,** the following are a few of the most popular and interesting. **'Abbotswood'** is one of the best white-flowered cultivars; **'Pink Beauty'** bears pink, semi-double flowers; **'Tangerine'** has orange flowers and **'Yellow Gem'** has bright yellow flowers.

Also called: shrubby cinquefoil **Features:** attractive flowers and foliage **Habit:** mounding, deciduous shrub **Flower color:** white, pink, orange, yellow, red **Height:** 12–60" **Spread:** 12–60" **Hardiness:** zones 2–8

Quince
Chaenomeles

Beautiful in flower, these plants create an attractive display when trained to grow up or along a brick wall.

Growing

Quince grows well in **full sun**. It tolerates partial shade but will produce fewer flowers. The soil should be of **average fertility, moist, slightly acidic** and **well drained**. These shrubs are tolerant of pollution and urban conditions.

Tips

Quinces can be included in shrub and mixed borders. They are very attractive when grown against a wall, and their spiny habit makes them useful for barriers. Use them along the edge of a woodland or in a naturalistic garden. The dark stems stand out well against the snow in winter.

C. speciosa 'Texas Scarlet' (above & below)

Recommended

C. japonica (Japanese flowering quince) is a spreading shrub that grows 24–36" tall and spreads up to 6'. Orange or red flowers are borne in early or mid-spring, followed by small, fragrant, greenish yellow fruit.

The fruits of quinces are edible when cooked.

C. speciosa (common flowering quince) is a large, tangled, spreading shrub. It grows 6–10' tall and spreads 6–15'. Red flowers are borne in spring, followed by fragrant, greenish yellow fruit. Many cultivars are available, including the popular **'Toyo-Nishiki'** that produces red, pink and white flowers all on the same plant.

Also called: flowering quince **Features:** spring flowers; fragrant fruit; habit **Habit:** spreading, deciduous shrub with spiny branches **Flower color:** red, pink, white, orange **Height:** 2–10' **Spread:** 2–15' **Hardiness:** zones 5–8

Redbud

Cercis

Redbud is an outstanding treasure of spring. Deep magenta flowers bloom before the leaves emerge, and their impact is intense. As the buds open, the flowers turn pink, covering the long, thin branches in pastel clouds.

Growing
Redbud will grow well in **full sun, partial shade** or **light shade**. The soil should be a **fertile, deep loam** that is **moist** and **well drained**. This plant has tender roots and does not like being transplanted.

Tips
Redbud can be used as a specimen tree, in a shrub or mixed border or in a woodland garden.

Recommended
C. canadensis (eastern redbud) is a spreading, multi-stemmed tree that bears red, purple or pink flowers. The young foliage is bronze, fading to green over the summer and turning bright yellow in fall. Many beautiful cultivars are available.

C. canadensis (above & below)

Redbud is not as long-lived as many other trees, so use its delicate beauty to supplement more permanent trees in the garden.

Features: spring flowers; fall foliage **Habit:** rounded or spreading, multi-stemmed, deciduous tree or shrub **Flower color:** red, purple, pink **Height:** 20–30' **Spread:** 25–35' **Hardiness:** zones 4–9

Serviceberry
Amelanchier

The *Amelanchier* species are first-rate North American natives, bearing lacy, white flowers in spring, followed by edible berries. In fall the foliage color ranges from a glowing apricot to deep red.

Growing
Serviceberries grow well in **full sun** or **light shade**. They prefer **acidic** soil that is **fertile, humus rich, moist** and **well drained**. They do adjust to drought.

Tips
With spring flowers, edible fruit, attractive leaves that turn red in fall and often artistic branch growth, serviceberries make beautiful specimen plants or even shade trees in small gardens. The shrubbier forms can be grown along the edges of a woodland or in a border. In the wild these trees are often found growing near water sources, and they are beautiful beside ponds or streams.

Recommended
Several species and hybrids are available. A few popular serviceberries are **A. arborea** (downy serviceberry, Juneberry), a small, single- or multi-stemmed tree; **A. canadensis** (shadblow serviceberry), a large, upright, suckering shrub; and **A. x grandiflora** (apple serviceberry), a small, spreading, often multi-stemmed tree. All three have white flowers, purple fruit and good fall color.

A. canadensis (above)

Serviceberry fruit can be used in place of blueberries in any recipe. The fruit has a similar but generally sweeter flavor.

Also called: saskatoon, Juneberry **Features:** spring or early-summer flowers; edible fruit; fall color; bark **Habit:** single- or multi-stemmed, deciduous, large shrub or small tree **Flower color:** white **Height:** 4–30' **Spread:** 4–30' **Hardiness:** zones 3–9

Seven-Son Flower
Heptacodium

H. miconioides (above)

A s a smallish tree with fragrant, white, fall flowers followed by red sepals and fruit, seven-son flower makes a welcome addition to our plant palette.

This plant is a fairly recent introduction to North American gardens and may not be available in all garden centers.

Growing

Seven-son flower prefers **full sun** but tolerates partial shade. The soil should be of **average fertility, moist** and **well drained,** though this plant is fairly tolerant of most soil conditions, including dry or acidic soil.

Tips

This large shrub can be used in place of a shade tree on a small property. Planted near a patio or deck, the plant will provide light shade, and its fragrant flowers can be enjoyed in late summer. In a border it provides light shade to plants growing below it, and the dark green leaves make a good backdrop for bright perennial and annual flowers.

Seven-son flower's tolerance of dry and salty soils makes it useful where salty snow may be shoveled off walkways in winter and where watering may be minimal in summer.

Recommended

H. miconioides is a large, multistemmed shrub or small tree with peeling, tan bark and dark green leaves that may become tinged with purple in fall. Clusters of fragrant, creamy white flowers have persistent sepals (the outer ring of flower parts) that turn dark pink to bright red in mid- to late fall and surround small, purple-red fruit.

Features: bark; fall flowers **Habit:** upright to spreading, multi-stemmed, deciduous shrub or small tree **Flower color:** white **Height:** 15–20' **Spread:** 8–15' **Hardiness:** zones 5–8

Silverbell

Halasia

These lovely, small trees deserve to be used more widely in the small gardens that are common in today's housing developments.

Growing

Silverbell grows well in **full sun, partial shade** or **light shade**. The soil should be **fertile, humus rich, neutral to acidic, moist** and **well drained**.

Tips

Silverbells make attractive, small to medium-sized specimen trees. They can also be used in a woodland garden or as backdrop plants in a shrub or mixed border.

Recommended

H. diptera (two-wing silverbell) is a small, rounded, often multi-stemmed tree that grows 20–30' tall, with an equal spread. It bears white flowers in early summer. The foliage turns yellow in fall.

H. tetraptera (snowdrop tree, Carolina silverbell, mountain silverbell) is a rounded, spreading tree. It grows 25–40' tall and spreads 25–35'. White flowers are borne in spring, before the leaves emerge. The foliage turns yellow in fall. A cultivar called **'Rosea'** bears flowers in variable shades of pink.

H. tetraptera (above & below)

Depending on the species, two or four narrow 'wings' (ridges) run down the length of each fruit capsule, giving rise to the specific epithets diptera, 'two-winged' and tetraptera, 'four-winged.'

Features: late-spring to early-summer flowers; attractive summer and fall foliage **Habit:** spreading, rounded, deciduous tree **Flower color:** white **Height:** 20–40' **Spread:** 20–35' **Hardiness:** zones 5–9

Smokebush

Cotinus

C. coggygria (above & below)

Bright fall color, adaptability, flowers of differing colors, and variable sizes and forms make smokebush and all its cultivars excellent additions to the garden.

Growing

Smokebush grows well in **full sun** or **partial shade**. It prefers soil of **average fertility** that is **moist** and **well drained,** but it will adapt to all but very wet soils.

Tips

Smokebush can be used in a shrub or mixed border, as a single specimen or in groups. It is a good choice for a rocky hillside planting.

Recommended

C. coggygria is a bushy, rounded shrub that develops large, puffy plumes of flowers that start out green and gradually turn a pinky gray. The green foliage turns red, orange and yellow in fall. Many cultivars are available, including purple-leaved varieties.

Try encouraging a clematis vine to wind its way through the spreading branches of a smokebush.

Also called: smoketree **Features:** attractive, early-summer flowers; summer and fall foliage **Habit:** bushy, rounded, spreading, deciduous tree or shrub **Flower color:** green, turning a pinky gray **Height:** 10–15' **Spread:** 10–15' **Hardiness:** zones 4–8

Spirea
Spiraea

S. x vanhouttei (above & below)

Spireas, seen in so many gardens and with dozens of cultivars, remain undeniable favorites. With a wide range of forms, sizes and colors of both foliage and flowers, spireas have many possible uses in the landscape.

Growing

Spireas prefer **full sun**. To help prevent foliage burn, provide protection from very hot sun. The soil should be **fertile, acidic, moist** and **well drained**.

Tips

Spireas are used in shrub or mixed borders, in rock gardens and as informal screens and hedges.

Recommended

Many species and cultivars of spirea are available. Two popular hybrid groups follow. **S. x bumalda** (*S. japonica* 'Bumalda') is a low, broad, mounded shrub with pink flowers. It is rarely grown in favor of the many cultivars, which also have pink flowers but have brightly colored foliage. **S. x vanhouttei** (bridal wreath spirea, Vanhoutte spirea) is a dense, bushy shrub with arching branches that bears clusters of white flowers. Check with your local nursery or garden center to see what is available.

Features: attractive, summer flowers; habit
Habit: round, bushy, deciduous shrub
Flower color: pink, white **Height:** 1–10'
Spread: 1–12' **Hardiness:** zones 3–9

Spruce
Picea

P. glauca 'Conica' (above),
P. pungens var. glauca 'Moerheim' (below)

The spruce is one of the most commonly grown and commonly abused evergreens. Grow spruces where they have enough room to spread and then let them branch all the way to the ground.

Growing
Spruce trees grow best in **full sun**. The soil should be **deep, moist, well drained** and **neutral to acidic**. These trees generally don't like hot, dry or polluted conditions. Spruces are best grown from small, young stock as they dislike being transplanted when larger or more mature.

Tips
Spruces are used as specimen trees. The dwarf and slow-growing cultivars can also be used in shrub or mixed borders. These trees look most attractive when allowed to keep their lower branches.

Recommended
Spruce are generally upright, pyramidal trees, but cultivars may be low growing, wide spreading or even weeping in habit. *P. abies* (Norway spruce), *P. glauca* (white spruce), *P. omorika* (Serbian spruce), *P. pungens* (Colorado spruce) and their cultivars are popular and commonly available.

Oil-based pesticides such as dormant oil can take the blue out of your blue-needled spruces. However, the new growth will have the blue coloring.

Features: foliage; cones **Habit:** conical or columnar, evergreen tree or shrub **Height:** 2–80' **Spread:** 2–25' **Hardiness:** zones 2–8

St. Johnswort

Hypericum

Masses of bright yellow flowers with numerous, showy, hair-like stamens add sunshine to the summer garden.

Growing

St. Johnsworts grow best in **full sun** but tolerate partial shade. **Well-drained** soil of **average fertility** is preferred, but these plants adapt to most soil conditions except wet soils. They also tolerate drought and heavy, rocky or very alkaline soils.

Tips

St. Johnsworts make good additions to mixed or shrub borders, where the late-summer flowers can brighten up a planting that is looking tired or faded in the heat of summer. These durable shrubs are also useful for difficult areas where the soil is poor and watering is difficult.

Recommended

H. frondosum (golden St. Johnswort) forms a rounded, upright mound. This deciduous species grows 2–4' tall, with an equal spread. Bright yellow flowers are borne in mid- and late summer. The long, dense stamens give each flower a fuzzy appearance. **'Sunburst'** is a frequently recommended cultivar. (Zones 5–8)

H. kalmianum (Kalm St. Johnswort) is a bushy, evergreen shrub that is

H. kalmianum 'Ames' (above)

native to Michigan. It grows 24–36" tall, with an equal spread. Yellow flowers are borne from mid- to late summer. Recommended cultivars include **'Ames'** and **'Gemo.'**

Many medicinal and magical properties have been attributed to species of St. Johnswort. It is currently used to treat mild forms of depression.

Also called: St. John's Wort **Features:** summer to fall flowers; attractive foliage **Habit:** tidy, rounded, deciduous or evergreen shrub **Flower color:** yellow **Height:** 2–4' **Spread:** 2–4' **Hardiness:** zones 4–8

Summersweet Clethra
Clethra

Summersweet clethra attracts butterflies and other pollinators and is one of the best shrubs for adding fragrance to your garden.

Growing

Summersweet clethra grows best in **light or partial shade**. The soil should be **fertile, humus rich, acidic, moist** and **well drained**. Dead head plants once flowering is complete to keep plants looking tidy. These plants require little if any pruning.

Tips

Although not aggressive, this shrub tends to sucker, forming a colony of stems. Use it in a border or in a woodland garden. The light shade along the edge of a woodland is also an ideal location.

Recommended

C. alnifolia is a large, rounded, upright, colony-forming shrub. It grows 3–8' tall, spreading 3–6' and bearing attractive spikes of white flowers in mid- to late summer. The foliage turns yellow in fall. Recommended cultivars include the low-growing **'Hummingbird'** and **'Ruby Spice,'** a selection with reddish pink flowers.

C. alnifolia 'September Beauty' (above),
C. alnifolia 'Panicalata' (below)

Summersweet clethra is useful in damp, shaded gardens, where the late-season flowers are much appreciated.

Also called: sweet pepperbush, sweetspire
Features: fragrant, summer flowers; attractive habit; colorful fall foliage **Habit:** rounded, suckering, deciduous shrub **Flower color:** white, reddish pink **Height:** 2–8' **Spread:** 3–8' **Hardiness:** zones 3–9

Thornless Honeylocust

Gleditsia

Thornless honeylocust remains a popular tree for lawn and street plantings, and the brilliant, deep yellow fall color is wonderful to behold.

Growing

Thornless honeylocust prefers **full sun**. The soil should be **fertile** and **well drained**. This tree adapts to most soil types.

Tips

Use thornless honeylocust as a specimen tree. Although it is often used as a street tree, this species is a poor choice for that purpose because the vigorous roots can break up pavement and sidewalks. Also, mass plantings (such as along a street) may lead to problems because the roots become entwined and diseases can quickly travel from one tree to another.

Recommended

G. triacanthos var. *inermis* is a spreading, rounded, thornless tree with inconspicuous flowers and sometimes long, pea-like pods that persist into fall. The autumn color is a warm, golden yellow. Many cultivars are available, including compact varieties, weeping varieties and varieties with bright yellow, spring foliage.

G. *triacanthos* var. *inermis* (above & below)

This adaptable, quick-growing tree provides very light shade, making it a good choice for lawns.

Features: summer and fall foliage **Habit:** rounded, spreading, deciduous tree **Height:** 15–100' **Spread:** 15–70' **Hardiness:** zones 4–8

Viburnum

Viburnum

V. opulus (above), V. plicatum (below)

Good fall color, attractive form, shade tolerance, scented flowers and attractive fruit put the viburnums in a class by themselves.

Growing

Viburnums grow well in **full sun, partial shade** or **light shade**. The soil should be of **average fertility, moist** and **well drained**. Viburnums tolerate both alkaline and acidic soils.

These plants will look neatest if deadheaded, but this practice will prevent fruits from forming. Fruiting is better when more than one plant of a species is grown.

Tips

Viburnums can be used in borders and woodland gardens. They are a good choice for plantings near swimming pools.

Recommended

Many viburnum species, hybrids and cultivars are available. A few popular ones include *V. carlesii* (Korean spice viburnum), a dense, bushy, rounded, deciduous shrub with white or pink, spicy-scented flowers (zones 5–8); *V. dentatum* (arrowwood), a shade-loving, upright shrub with blue fruit (zones 3–7); *V. opulus* (European cranberrybush, Guelder-rose), a rounded, spreading, deciduous shrub with lacy-looking flower clusters (zones 3–8); *V. plicatum* var. *tomentosum* (doublefile viburnum), with a graceful, horizontal branching pattern, which gives the shrub a layered effect, and lacy-looking, white flower clusters (zones 5–8); and *V. trilobum* (American cranberrybush, highbush cranberry), a dense, rounded shrub with clusters of white flowers, followed by edible, red fruit (zones 2–7).

The edible but very tart fruits of V. opulus *and* V. trilobum *are popular for making jellies, pies and wine. They can be sweetened somewhat by freezing or by picking them after the first frost or two.*

Features: attractive flowers (some fragrant); summer and fall foliage; fruit **Habit:** bushy or spreading, evergreen, semi-evergreen or deciduous shrub **Flower color:** white, pink **Height:** 1½–20' **Spread:** 1½–15' **Hardiness:** zones 2–8

Weigela
Weigela

Weigelas have been improved through breeding, and specimens with more compact forms, longer flowering periods and greater cold tolerance are now available.

Growing
Weigela prefers **full sun** but tolerates partial shade. The soil should be **fertile** and **well drained**. This plant will adapt to most well-drained soil conditions.

Tips
Weigelas can be used in shrub or mixed borders, in open woodland gardens and as informal barrier plantings.

Recommended
W. florida is a spreading shrub with arching branches that bears clusters of dark pink flowers. Many hybrids and cultivars are available. Some of the best selections include **'Carnaval,'** with red, white or pink, thick azalea-like flowers; MIDNIGHT WINE, a low-mounding dwarf with dark burgundy foliage; **'Polka,'** with bright pink flowers; **'Red Prince,'** with dark red flowers; **'Rubidor,'** with yellow foliage and red flowers; **'Variegata,'** with yellow-green variegated foliage and pink flowers; and WINE AND ROSES, with dark burgundy foliage and rosy-pink colored flowers.

W. Florida 'Polka' (above), *W. florida* cultivar (below)

Weigela is one of the longest-blooming shrubs, with the main flush of blooms lasting as long as six weeks. It often re-blooms if sheared lightly after the first flowers fade.

Features: late-spring to early-summer flowers; foliage **Habit:** upright or low, spreading, deciduous shrub **Flower color:** red, white, pink **Height:** 1–9' **Spread:** 1–12' **Hardiness:** zones 3–8

White Forsythia
Abeliophyllum

A. distichum (above & below)

Blooming shrubs such as white forsythia are a welcome sight in early spring, signaling that a long winter is finally over.

Growing
White forsythia prefers **full sun** but tolerates very light shade. The soil should be of **average fertility** and **well drained,** but this shrub adapts to most well-drained soils.

Tips
White forsythia tends to become a tangled mass of twigs, but the showy, early-spring flowers make up for its deficiencies when not in bloom. Include this plant in a planting with true forsythia, witchhazel and crocuses to create a wonderful, early-season show. White forsythia can also be included in a sunny border or in a naturalized garden.

Recommended
A. distichum is a spreading, suckering shrub that bears creamy white flowers in late winter or early spring. The foliage may turn purple in fall. A pink-flowered cultivar called **'Roseum'** is available.

These plants will survive in zone 4, but flower buds not protected with a layer of snow may be killed.

Also called: Korean abelialeaf **Features:** late-winter or early-spring flowers **Habit:** deciduous shrub **Flower color:** pink, white **Height:** 3–5' **Spread:** 3–5' **Hardiness:** zones 5–8

Witchhazel

Hamamelis

Witchhazel is an investment in happiness. It blooms in early spring, the flowers last for weeks and their spicy fragrance awakens the senses. Then in fall, the handsome leaves develop overlapping bands of orange, yellow and red.

Growing

Witchhazel grows best in a sheltered spot with **full sun** or **light shade**. The soil should be of **average fertility, neutral to acidic, moist** and **well drained**.

Tips

Witchhazels work well individually or in groups. They can be used as specimen plants, in shrub or mixed borders or in woodland gardens. As small trees, they are ideal for space-limited gardens.

The unique flowers have long, narrow, crinkled petals that give the plant a spidery appearance when in bloom. If the weather gets too cold, the petals will roll up, protecting the flowers and extending the flowering season.

Recommended

H. x *intermedia* is a vase-shaped, spreading shrub that bears fragrant clusters of yellow, orange or red flowers.

The leaves turn attractive shades of orange, red and bronze in fall. Cultivars with flowers in shades of red, yellow or orange are available.

Witchhazel branches can be cut and forced into bloom indoors in winter.

Features: fragrant, early-spring flowers; attractive summer and fall foliage **Habit:** spreading, deciduous shrub or small tree **Flower color:** red, yellow, orange **Height:** 6–20' **Spread:** 6–20' **Hardiness:** zones 5–8

Woadwaxen

Genista

G. *lydia* (above & below)

Of planted where they can grow over the top of a low retaining wall, these low-growing plants look like bright yellow waterfalls when in flower.

Growing

Woadwaxen prefers **full sun** in a **warm, sheltered location**. The soil should be of **average to low fertility, sandy or gravely** and **well drained**. Although this plant tolerates dry soil and adapts to most soils, it prefers alkaline soil. These shrubs resent being transplanted and should not be moved once they are established.

Tips

The taller species of woadwaxen can be used in a shrub border. The groundcover species can be used in rock gardens and along the tops of rock walls. All species can be used to prevent erosion on exposed slopes.

Recommended

G. lydia is a mounding, groundcover plant that generally grows about 24" tall and spreads about 36". It bears bright yellow flowers in early summer. Some frost damage may occur on plants in areas colder than zone 6 if snow cover is poor. (Zones 4–9)

These plants are members of the pea family, though, as is often the case, the fruit is not edible.

Also called: broom, greenwood **Features:** flowers; bright green stems **Habit:** low, deciduous shrub **Flower color:** yellow **Height:** 2–6' **Spread:** 3–7' **Hardiness:** zones 3–9

Yellowwood

Cladrastis

This lovely shade tree is appealing in all seasons—with spring flowers, summer and fall foliage, and smooth, gray bark and a pleasing form that stand out in winter.

Growing

Yellowwood grows best in **full sun**. The soil should be **fertile, moist** and **well drained**. **Alkaline** soil is preferred, but this plant adapts to soil of any pH. These trees resent having their roots disturbed, so plant them when they are young and don't try to move them again.

Tips

Yellowwood is a beautiful, flowering, shade tree appropriate for medium to large properties. Avoid planting this tree near houses or other buildings because the wood is fairly weak and branches may break off in a strong wind.

Recommended

C. lutea (*C. kentukea*) is an attractive, wide-spreading tree with bright, yellowish green leaves. In late spring and early summer, the branches are covered with long, drooping clusters of white or pink, pea-like flowers.

C. lutea (above & below)

Foliage turns bright yellow in fall. The bark is smooth and gray, much like beech bark.

The genus name Cladrastis *comes from the Greek* klados, *'branch,' and* thraustos, *'fragile,' referring to the brittle wood of this tree.*

Also called: American yellowwood
Features: attractive, summer and fall foliage; spring flowers **Habit:** rounded, low-branching, deciduous tree **Flower color:** white, pink
Height: 30–50' **Spread:** 30–55'
Hardiness: zones 4–8

Yew

Taxus

T. x media 'Sunburst' (above), T. cuspidata (below)

From sweeping hedges to commanding specimens, yews can serve many purposes in the garden. They are the only reliable evergreens for deep shade.

Growing

Yews grow well in any light conditions, from **full sun to full shade**. The soil should be fertile, **moist** and **well drained**. These trees tolerate windy, dry and polluted conditions, and soils of any acidity. They dislike excessive heat, however, and on the hotter south or southwest side of a building they may suffer needle scorch.

Tips

Yews can be used in borders or as specimens, hedges, topiaries and groundcovers.

Male and female flowers are borne on separate plants. Both must be present for the attractive red arils (seed cups) to form.

Recommended

T. x media (English Japanese yew), a cross between *T. baccata* (English yew) and *T. cuspidata* (Japanese yew), has the vigor of the English yew and the cold hardiness of the Japanese yew. It forms a rounded, upright tree or shrub, though the size and form can vary among the many cultivars, such as the globe-shaped **'Brownii,'** the columnar **'Hisksii'** and the low-spreading **'Tautonii.'**

All parts of yew are poisonous except the edible, fleshy red aril that surrounds the inedible seed.

Features: attractive foliage and red seed cups **Habit:** evergreen; conical or columnar tree, or bushy or spreading shrub **Height:** 1–70' **Spread:** 1–30' **Hardiness:** zones

Altissimo

Climbing Floribunda Rose

*I*talian for 'in the highest,' Altissimo is an apt name for this high-climbing, high-quality, highly disease-resistant rose.

Growing

Altissimo grows best in **full sun, in a warm, sheltered location**. The soil should be **fertile, slightly acidic, humus rich, moist** and **well drained**. The canes must be attached to a sturdy support.

Tips

Altissimo's stiff, sturdy stems form a bushy, spreading plant that can be grown as a large shrub or trained to climb a wall, trellis, porch or pergola.

Recommended

Rosa 'Altissimo' has large, matte, serrated, leathery, dark green foliage and single flowers that are borne in clusters for most of the growing season on both new and old growth. In a warm location Altissimo can grow to cover a wall but in Michigan it generally grows smaller.

When cut, the long-stemmed blooms are long lasting and unfading. They can be used in a variety of arrangements.

George Delbard of Delbard-Chabert developed Altissimo in 1966 in France. It was a seedling of Tenor, a red climber created by Delbard.

Also called: Altus, Sublimely Single
Features: vigorous climber; slightly clove-scented, early summer to fall flowers
Flower color: blood red **Height:** 8–9'
Spread: 5–8' **Hardiness:** zones 5–9

Carefree Delight

Modern Shrub Rose

The name of this shrub rose is perfectly appropriate—it requires very little care and produces copious quantities of flowers in waves throughout summer.

Growing

Carefree Delight prefers **full sun** but tolerates some shade. The soil should be **average to fertile, humus rich, slightly acidic, moist** and **well drained,** but this rose has proven to be quite adaptable to a variety of soil conditions. Carefree Delight is disease resistant.

Tips

Carefree Delight makes a good addition to a mixed bed or border, and it is attractive when planted in groups of three or more. It can be mass planted to create a large display, or grown singly as an equally attractive specimen.

Recommended

Rosa **'Carefree Delight'** is a bushy, rounded shrub with dark green, glossy foliage that turns bronzy red in fall. Large clusters of single, pink flowers with white or yellow centers and contrasting yellow stamens are borne for most of the summer. There are several other roses in the **Carefree Series,** including **'Carefree Beauty,'** with medium pink, double flowers, and **'Carefree Sunshine,'** with yellow flowers.

Carefree Delight is consistent in all climates, making it suitable for just about any setting or region.

Features: rounded habit; summer and fall foliage; long blooming period; attractive hips; disease resistant **Flower color:** yellow; carmine pink with a white center **Height:** 3–4' **Spread:** 3–4' **Hardiness:** zones 4–9

Flower Carpet

Groundcover Rose

Since their release in 1991, Flower Carpet roses have proven themselves to be low-maintenance, black spot-resistant and long-blooming performers in the landscape.

Growing

Flower Carpet roses grow best in **full sun.** The soil should be **average to fertile, humus rich, slightly acidic, moist** and **well drained,** but this hardy rose is fairly adaptable.

Tips

Although not true groundcovers, these small shrub roses have dense and spreading habits that are useful for filling in large areas. They can also be used as low hedges or in mixed borders. Their sometimes long, rangy canes may require some pruning to reduce their spread. Flower Carpet roses even grow well near roads, sidewalks and driveways where salt is applied in winter.

Recommended

Rosa 'Flower Carpet' roses are bushy, low-growing, spreading plants with shiny, bright green, leathery foliage. They produce single or semi-double flowers in white, yellow, pink, coral, red, or apple blossom, with prominent, yellow stamens.

These flowers last from early summer through fall, to the first heavy frost.

Features: mounding, spreading habit; summer through fall flowers **Flower color:** pink, white, yellow, coral, red, apple blossom **Height:** 30–36" **Spread:** 3–4" **Hardiness:** zones 5–9

Hansa

Rugosa Shrub Rose

Hansa, first introduced in 1905, is one of the most durable, long-lived and versatile roses.

Growing

Hansa grows best in **full sun**. The soil should preferably be **average to fertile, humus rich, slightly acidic, moist** and **well drained,** but this durable rose adapts to most soils, from sandy to silty clay. Remove a few of the oldest canes every few years to keep plants blooming vigorously.

Tips

Rugosa roses such as Hansa make good additions to mixed borders and beds, and can also be used as hedges or as specimens. They are often used on steep banks to prevent soil erosion. Their prickly branches deter people from walking across flower beds and compacting the soil.

Recommended

Rosa 'Hansa' is a bushy shrub with arching canes and leathery, deeply veined, bright green leaves. The double flowers are produced all summer. The bright orange hips persist into winter. Other rugosa roses include **'Blanc Double de Coubert,'** which produces white, double flowers all summer.

Hansa is a wide-spreading plant with disease-resistant foliage; this disease resistance is commonly found in rugosa roses.

Features: dense, arching habit; clove-scented, early summer to fall flowers; orange-red hips **Flower color:** mauve purple or mauve red **Height:** 4–5' **Spread:** 5–6' **Hardiness:** zones 3–9

Hope For Humanity

Parkland Shrub Rose

Introduced in 1995, Hope for Humanity was named in honor of the 100th anniversary of the Canadian Red Cross Society.

Growing

Hope for Humanity grows best in **full sun**. The soil should be **fertile, humus rich, slightly acidic, moist** and **well drained**. Its foliage is resistant to mildew and rust but is somewhat susceptible to black spot.

Tips

This small plant makes a good addition to a mixed bed or border, and it is especially attractive when planted in groups of three or more. Its small stature also makes it a popular choice for containers and large planters, though some winter protection may be needed for plants not grown directly in the ground.

Recommended

Rosa '**Hope for Humanity**' is a compact, low-growing shrub with glossy, dark green foliage and double flowers produced over a long period in summer. The Parkland rose series boasts a wide range of flower colors, some of which are uncommon in hardy shrub roses.

The hardy Parkland roses were developed in Brandon, Manitoba, for use in prairie gardens to withstand the cold winters.

Features: compact habit; lightly scented, mid-summer to fall flowers **Flower color:** blood red with small white spot at petal base and a white or yellow spot on the outer margin of each petal **Height:** 24" **Spread:** 24" **Hardiness:** zones 3–8

Knockout

Modern Shrub Rose

This rose is simply one of the best new shrub roses to hit the market in years.

Growing

Knockout grows best in **full sun**. The soil should be **fertile, humus rich, slightly acidic, moist** and **well drained**. This rose blooms most prolifically in warm weather but has deeper red flowers in cooler weather. Deadhead lightly to keep the plant tidy and to encourage prolific blooming.

Tips

This vigorous rose makes a good addition to a mixed bed or border, and it is attractive when planted in groups of three or more. It can be mass planted to create a large display, or grown singly as an equally beautiful specimen.

Recommended

Rosa 'Knockout' has a lovely, rounded form with glossy, green leaves that turn to shades of burgundy in fall. The bright, cherry red flowers are borne in clusters of 3–15 almost all summer and into fall. Orange-red hips last well into winter. **'Double Knockout,' 'Pink Knockout'** and a light pink selection called **'Blushing Knockout'** are all available. All have excellent disease resistance.

If you've been afraid that roses need too much care, you'll appreciate the hardiness and disease resistance of this low-maintenance beauty.

Also called: Knock Out **Features:** rounded habit; light, tea rose scented, mid-summer to fall flowers; disease resistant **Flower color:** cherry red, pink **Height:** 3–4' **Spread:** 3–4' **Hardiness:** zones 4–10

Queen Elizabeth

Grandiflora Rose

The grandiflora classification was originally created to accommodate this rose. Queen Elizabeth is one of the most widely grown and best-loved roses.

Growing

Queen Elizabeth grows best in **full sun**. The soil should be **average to fertile, humus rich, slightly acidic, moist** and **well drained,** but this durable rose adapts to most soils and tolerates high heat and humidity. Prune plants back to 5–7 canes and 5–7 buds each spring.

Tips

Queen Elizabeth is a trouble-free rose that makes a good addition to mixed borders and beds. It can also be used as a specimen, to form a hedge or grown in a large planter. Its flowers are borne on sturdy stems that make them useful for floral arrangements.

Recommended

Rosa 'Queen Elizabeth' is a bushy shrub with glossy, dark green foliage and dark stems. The pink, cup-shaped, double flowers may be borne singly or in clusters of several flowers.

Queen Elizabeth has won many honors and was named World's Favorite Rose in 1979.

Features: glossy, dark green, disease-resistant foliage; lightly scented, summer to fall flowers **Flower color:** soft, pearly pink **Height:** 4–6' **Spread:** 30–36" **Hardiness:** zones 5–9

Rosa Glauca

Species Rose

This species rose is a gardener's dream—it's hardy, has good disease resistance, and has striking foliage in summer and colorful hips in winter.

Growing

Rosa glauca grows best and develops contrasting foliage color in **full sun** but tolerates some shade. The soil should be **average to fertile, humus rich, slightly acidic, moist** and **well drained,** but this rose adapts to most soils, from sandy soil to silty clay.

Remove a few of the oldest canes to the ground every few years to encourage younger, more colorful stems to grow in. Removing spent flowers won't prolong the blooming period, and the more flowers you leave, the more hips will form.

Tips

With its unusual foliage color, *Rosa glauca* makes a good addition to mixed borders and beds, and it can also be used as a hedge or specimen.

Recommended

Rosa glauca (*R. rubrifolia*) is a bushy shrub with arching, purple-tinged canes and delicate, purple-tinged, blue-green leaves. The single, star-like flowers bloom in clusters in late spring. The dark red hips persist until spring.

Rosa glauca is extremely popular with rosarians and novice gardeners alike because of its hardiness, disease resistance, dainty blooms and foliage color. It received the Royal Horticultural Society Award of Garden Merit—proof of its dependable performance.

Also called: red-leafed rose **Features:** dense, arching habit; purple- or red-tinged foliage; late-spring flowers; persistent dark red hips **Flower color:** mauve pink with white centers **Height:** 6–10' **Spread:** 5–6' **Hardiness:** zones 2–9

Rosemary Harkness

Hybrid Tea Rose

Rosemary Harkness is often the first rose to bloom in late spring or early summer.

Growing

Rosemary Harkness grows best in **full sun** in a **warm, sheltered location**. The soil should be **fertile, humus rich, slightly acidic, moist** and **well drained**. This rose likes a very fertile soil; amending the soil with additional **organic matter** will improve its nutrient content, texture, water retention and drainage. Winter protection will increase this rose's chance of overwintering successfully.

Tips

Rosemary Harkness, with its stunning flowers, is best used as a specimen plant but can be used in a mixed border with shallow-rooted plants that will not compete excessively for water and nutrients. Plant it where you can enjoy its fragrant flowers.

Recommended

Rosa **'Rosemary Harkness'** is a vigorous, shrubby rose with glossy, dark green leaves. It produces fully double flowers all summer.

These beautiful, uniquely colored flowers are a welcome addition to any flower arrangement and are sure to become a conversation piece.

Also called: harrowbond **Features:** spreading habit; sweet, fruity-scented, late spring to fall flowers **Flower color:** apricot yellow with salmon pink edges **Height:** 30" **Spread:** 30" **Hardiness:** zones 6–9

The Fairy

Polyantha Rose

The Fairy is popular with gardeners of all skill levels, from novice to experienced, for its ease of care, long blooming period and lovely flowers.

Growing

The Fairy grows best in **full sun**. The soil should be **fertile, humus rich, slightly acidic, moist** and **well drained**. Some pruning in spring may be required to control the spread of this rose.

The Fairy is trouble-free and resistant to disease, though spider mites may cause trouble during hot, dry weather.

Tips

The Fairy can be planted in containers, as a groundcover, or to trail over the top of a low wall or embankment. It is easily trained to form a weeping standard and blends nicely into mixed beds and borders. Plant in groups for a mass planting or an informal hedge.

Recommended

Rosa 'The Fairy' is a low, mound-forming shrub with arching branches. The foliage is glossy green. Pink, double flowers are borne in large clusters from mid-summer to frost.

Also called: Fairy, Feerie **Features:** spreading habit; long blooming period; flowers **Flower color:** soft pink **Height:** 24–36" **Spread:** 24–48" **Hardiness:** zones 4–9

Clematis

Clematis

There are so many species, hybrids and cultivars of clematis that it is possible to have one in bloom all season.

Growing

Clematis plants prefer **full sun** but tolerate partial shade. The soil should be **fertile, humus rich, moist** and **well drained**. These vines enjoy warm, sunny weather, but the roots prefer to be cool. A thick layer of mulch or a planting of low, shade-providing perennials will protect the tender roots. The rootball of vining clematis should be planted about 2" beneath the surface of the soil. Clematis are quite cold hardy but fare best when protected from winter wind.

Tips

Clematis vines can climb up structures such as trellises, railings, fences and arbors. They can also be allowed to grow over shrubs and up trees and can be used as groundcover.

Recommended

There are many species, hybrids and cultivars of clematis. The flower forms, blooming times and sizes of the plants can vary. Check with your local garden center to see what is available.

C. 'Etoile Violette' (above),
C. 'Gravetye Beauty' (below)

Plant two clematis varieties that bloom at the same time to provide a mix of color and texture.

Features: twining habit; early to late-summer flowers; decorative seedheads **Flower color:** blue, purple, pink, yellow, red, white **Height:** 10–17' or more **Spread:** 5' or more **Hardiness:** zones 3–8

Climbing Hydrangea

Hydrangea

H. anomala subsp. *petiolaris* (above & below)

A mature climbing hydrangea can cover an entire wall, and with its dark, glossy leaves and delicate, lacy flowers, it is quite possibly one of the most stunning climbing plants available.

Growing

Hydrangeas prefer **partial or light shade** but tolerate both full sun and full shade. The soil should be of **average to high fertility, humus rich, moist** and **well drained**. These plants perform best in cool, moist conditions, so be sure to mulch their roots.

Tips

Climbing hydrangea climbs up trees, walls, fences, pergolas and arbors. It clings to walls by means of aerial roots, so needs no support, just a somewhat textured surface. It also grows over rocks, can be used as a groundcover and can be trained to form a small tree or shrub.

Recommended

H. anomala subsp. *petiolaris* (*H. petiolaris*) is a clinging vine with dark, glossy green leaves that sometimes turn an attractive yellow in fall. For more than a month in mid-summer, the vine is covered with white, lacy-looking flowers, and the entire plant appears to be veiled in a lacy mist.

Features: flowers; clinging habit; exfoliating bark **Flower color:** white **Height:** 50–80' **Spread:** 50–80' **Hardiness:** zones 4–9

Fleece Vine

Polygonum

This charming vine is perfect for softening the edges of wooden structures such as deck lattice work and fences.

Growing

Fleece vine grows well in **full sun, partial shade** or **light shade**. The soil should be of **average to poor fertility, moist** and **well drained**. This plant requires a sturdy support to twine around.

Tips

This vine is useful for creating fast-growing screens, especially on chain-link fences. It can also be trained up an arbor, pergola or trellis.

Recommended

P. aubertii (*Fallopia aubertii*) is a fast-growing, twining, woody climber. The clusters of small, white flowers are produced in late summer and stand out attractively against the heart-shaped leaves. This vigorous grower can overwhelm other plants so make sure you place it where it can grow up a sturdy structure and not over neighboring plants.

P. aubertii (above & below)

Fleece vine roots where its branches touch the ground, and new plants can sprout from small pieces of root left in the ground.

Also called: mile-a-minute plant, silver lace vine **Features:** twining, deciduous vine; attractive summer flowers and foliage **Flower color:** white **Height:** 25–40' or more **Spread:** 25–40' or more **Hardiness:** zones 4–8

Hardy Kiwi

Actinidia

A. arguta 'Ananasaya' (above), A. arguta (below)

Tips

These vines need a sturdy structure to twine around. Pergolas, arbors and sufficiently large and sturdy fences provide good support. Given a trellis against a wall, a tree or some other upright structure, hardy kiwis will twine upward all summer. They can also be grown in large containers.

Hardy kiwi vines can grow uncontrollably. Don't be afraid to prune them back if they are getting out of hand.

Recommended

There are two hardy kiwi vines commonly grown in cold-climate gardens. ***A. arguta*** (hardy kiwi, bower actinidia) has dark green, heart-shaped leaves, white flowers and smooth-skinned, greenish yellow, edible fruit. ***A. kolomikta*** (variegated kiwi vine, kolomikta actinidia) has green leaves strongly variegated with pink and white, white flowers and smooth-skinned, greenish yellow, edible fruit.

Hardy kiwi is handsome in its simplicity, and its lush green leaves, vigor and adaptability make it very useful, especially on difficult sites.

Growing

Hardy kiwi vines grow best in **full sun**. The soil should be **fertile** and **well drained**. These plants require **shelter from strong winds**.

Both a male and a female vine must be present for fruit to be produced. The plants are often sold in pairs.

Features: early-summer flowers; edible fruit; twining habit **Flower color:** white **Height:** 15–30' to indefinite **Spread:** 15–30' to indefinite **Hardiness:** zones 3–7

Honeysuckle

Lonicera

Honeysuckles can be rampant twining vines but with careful consideration and placement they won't overrun your garden. The fragrance of the flowers makes any effort worthwhile.

Growing

Honeysuckles grow well in **full sun** or **partial shade**. The soil should be **average to fertile, humus rich, moist** and **well drained**.

Tips

Honeysuckle can be trained to grow up a trellis, fence, arbor or other structure. In a large container near a porch it will ramble over the edges of the pot and up the railings with reckless abandon.

Recommended

There are dozens of honeysuckle species, hybrids and cultivars. Check with your local garden center to see what is available. The following are two popular species.

L. sempervirens (trumpet honeysuckle, coral honeysuckle) bears orange or red flowers in late spring and early summer. Many cultivars and hybrids are available with flowers in yellow, red or scarlet, including *L.* x *brownii* 'Dropmore Scarlet,' one of the hardiest of the climbing honeysuckles, cold hardy to zone 4.

L. x *brownii* 'Dropmore Scarlet' (above & below)

It bears bright red flowers for most of summer.

L. caprifolium (Italian honeysuckle, Italian woodbine) bears fragrant, creamy white or yellow flowers in late spring and early summer.

Features: late-spring and early-summer flowers; twining habit; fruit **Flower color:** creamy white, yellow, orange, red, scarlet **Height:** 6–20' **Spread:** 6–20' **Hardiness:** zones 5–9

Hops
Humulus

H. lupulus 'Aureus' (above), *H. lupulus* (below)

If you sit near hops for an afternoon, you might actually be able to watch the plant grow.

Growing

Hops grow best in **full sun**. The soil should be **average to fertile, humus rich, moist** and **well drained**, though established plants will adapt to most conditions as long as they are watered well for the first few years.

Hops are true perennials; each year the plant sends up shoots from ground level. The previous year's growth will need to be cleared away each fall or spring.

Tips

Hops will quickly twine around any sturdy support to create a screen or to shade a patio or deck. Provide a pergola, arbor, porch rail or even a telephone pole for hops to grow up. Most trellises are too delicate for this vigorous grower.

Recommended

H. lupulus is a fast-growing, twining vine with rough-textured, bright green leaves and stems. The fragrant, cone-like flowers are pale green and ripen to beige. The flowers are produced only on the female plants and are used to flavor beer. A cultivar with golden yellow foliage is available.

Features: twining habit; dense growth; cone-like, late-summer flowers **Flower color:** pale green ripening to beige **Height:** 10–20' **Spread:** 10–20' **Hardiness:** zones 3–8

Hydrangea Vine

Schizophragma

S. hydrangeoides (above), *S. hydrangeoides* 'Roseum' (below)

This vine is similar in appearance to climbing hydrangea but has a few interesting cultivars that add variety.

Growing

Hydrangea vine grows well in **full sun** or **partial shade**. The soil should be **average to fertile, humus rich, moist** and **well drained**.

This vine has trouble clinging to a smooth-surfaced wall. Attach a few supports to the wall and tie the vines to the supports. The dense growth will eventually hide the support.

Tips

Hydrangea vine clings to any rough surface and looks attractive climbing a wall, fence, tree, pergola or arbor. This vine can also be used as a groundcover on a bank or be allowed to grow up or over a rock wall.

Recommended

S. hydrangeoides is an attractive, climbing vine similar in appearance to climbing hydrangea. It bears lacy clusters of white flowers in mid-summer. **'Moonlight'** has silvery blue foliage. **'Roseum'** bears clusters of pink flowers.

Also called: Japanese hydrangea vine
Features: clinging habit; dark green or silvery foliage; flowers **Flower color:** white, pink **Height:** up to 40' **Spread:** up to 40' **Hardiness:** zones 5–8

Trumpet Vine
Campsis

C. radicans (above), *C. x tagliabuana* (below)

Trumpet vine is a fast-growing, twining vine that will cover just about any structure in less than five years.

Growing

These heat-tolerant vines grow well in full sun, partial shade or light shade but flower best in **full sun**. They will grow in any soil but growth is most rampant the more fertile the soil.

Tips

Trumpet vine will cling to any surface—a wall, a tree, a fence or a telephone pole. Once you have one of these vines you will probably never get rid of it. One plant can provide a privacy screen quickly or can be grown up an exterior wall or over the porch of a house. Trumpet vine can be used on arbors and trellises but will need frequent pruning to keep it looking its best and confined to the spot where you want it to grow.

Recommended

C. radicans is a fast-growing vine that bears dark orange, trumpet-shaped flowers for a long period in summer. Cultivars with red or yellow flowers are available.

C. x tagliabuana is similar in habit and size to *C. radicans* but is not as hardy or as aggressive. It bears bright orange flowers in summer. Plant this vine in a sheltered spot to protect it from cold, drying winter winds. **'Madame Galen'** is hardy to zone 5 and blooms prolifically. (Zones 6–9)

The trumpet-shaped flowers might attract hummingbirds to your garden.

Also called: trumpet creeper **Features:** clinging habit; summer flowers **Flower color:** orange, red, yellow **Height:** 30–60' **Spread:** 30–60' **Hardiness:** zones 4–9

Virginia Creeper / Boston Ivy

Parthenocissus

Virginia creeper and Boston ivy are handsome vines that establish quickly and provide an air of age and permanence, even on new structures.

Growing

These vines grow well in any light, from **full sun to full shade**. The soil should be **fertile** and **well drained**. The plants will adapt to clay or sandy soils.

Tips

Virginia creeper and Boston ivy can cover an entire building, given enough time. They do not require support because they have cling- ing rootlets that can adhere to just about any surface. They thrive on brick walls but will also climb smooth wood, vinyl or metal surfaces. Give the plants a lot of space and let them cover a wall, fence or arbor.

Recommended

These two species are very similar, except for the shape of the leaves.

P. quinquefolia (Virginia creeper, woodbine) has dark green foliage. Each leaf, divided into five leaflets, turns flame red in fall.

P. quinquefolia (above & below)

P. tricuspidata (Boston ivy, Japanese creeper) has dark green, three-lobed leaves that turn bright red in fall. This species is not quite as hardy as Vir- ginia creeper. (Zones 4–9)

These vines can cover the sides of buildings and help keep them cool in the summer heat. Cut the plants back to keep windows and doors accessible.

Features: summer and fall foliage; clinging habit **Height:** 30–70' **Spread:** 30–70' **Hardiness:** zones 3–9

Wisteria

Wisteria

W. *sinensis* (above & below)

Loose clusters of purple hang like lace from the branches of wisteria. A gardener willing to use garden shears can create beautiful tree forms and attractive arbor specimens.

The seeds in the long bean-like pods, along with all other parts of these plants, are poisonous.

Growing

Wisterias grow well in **full sun** or **partial shade**. The soil should be of **average fertility, moist** and **well drained**. Vines grown in too fertile a soil will produce a lot of vegetative growth but very few flowers. Avoid planting wisteria near a lawn where fertilizer may leach over to your vine.

Tips

These vines require something to twine around, such as an arbor or other sturdy structure. You can also train a wisteria to form a small tree. Try to select a permanent site; wisterias don't like being moved. These vigorous vines may send up suckers and can root wherever their branches touch the ground.

Recommended

W. *floribunda* (Japanese wisteria) bears long, pendulous clusters of fragrant, blue, purple, pink or white flowers in late spring before the leaves emerge. Long, bean-like pods follow.

W. *sinensis* (Chinese wisteria) bears long, pendent clusters of fragrant, blue-purple flowers in late spring. **'Alba'** has white flowers.

Features: late-spring flowers; foliage; twining habit **Flower color:** purple, blue, pink, white **Height:** 20–50' or more **Spread:** 20–50' or more **Hardiness:** zones 4–9

Canna Lily

Canna

Canna lilies are stunning, dramatic plants that give an exotic flair to any garden.

Growing

Canna lilies grow best in **full sun** in a **sheltered** location. The soil should be **fertile, moist** and **well drained**. Plant out in spring once the soil has warmed. Plants can be started early indoors in containers to get a head start on the growing season. Deadhead to prolong blooming.

Tips

Canna lilies can be grown in a bed or border. They make dramatic specimen plants and can even be included in large planters.

Recommended

A wide range of canna lilies are available, including cultivars and hybrids with green, bronzy, purple or yellow-and-green-striped foliage. Dwarf cultivars that grow 18–28" tall are also available.

'Red King Hambert' (below)

The rhizomes can be lifted after the foliage is killed back in fall. Clean off any clinging dirt and store them in a cool, frost-free location in slightly moist peat moss. Check on them regularly through the winter and if they start to sprout, pot them and move them to a bright window until they can be moved outdoors.

Features: decorative foliage; summer flowers
Flower color: white, red. orange, pink, yellow, bicolored **Height:** 3–6' **Spread:** 20–36" **Hardiness:** zones 7–9; grown as an annual

Crocus

Crocus

C. vernus cultivars (above & below)

Crocuses are harbingers of spring. They often appear, as if by magic, in full bloom from beneath the melting snow.

Growing

Crocuses grow well in **full sun** or **light, dappled shade**. The soil should be of **poor to average fertility, gritty** and **well drained**. The corms should be planted about 4" deep in fall.

Tips

Crocuses are almost always planted in groups. Drifts of crocuses can be planted in lawns to provide interest and color while the grass still lies dormant. They can be left to naturalize in beds or borders. Groups of plants will fill in and spread out to provide a bright welcome in spring.

Recommended

Many crocus species, hybrids and cultivars are available. The spring-flowering crocus most people are familiar with is **C. x *vernus***, commonly called Dutch crocus. Many cultivars are available with flowers in shades of purple, yellow and white, sometimes bicolored or with darker veins.

Saffron is obtained from the dried, crushed stigmas of C. sativus. Six plants produce enough spice for one recipe. This fall-blooming plant is hardy to zone 6 and can be grown successfully in the mildest parts of Michigan.

Features: early-spring flowers **Flower color:** purple, yellow, white, bicolored **Height:** 2–6" **Spread:** 2–4" **Hardiness:** zones 3–8

Daffodil

Narcissus

Many gardeners automatically think of large, yellow, trumpet-shaped flowers when they think of daffodils, but there is a lot of variety in color, form and size among the daffodils.

Growing

Daffodils grow best in **full sun** or **light, dappled shade**. The soil should be **average to fertile, moist** and **well drained**. Bulbs should be planted in fall, 2–8" deep, depending on the size of the bulb. The bigger the bulb, the deeper it should be planted. A rule of thumb is to measure the bulb from top to bottom and multiply that number by three to know how deeply to plant.

Tips

Daffodils are often planted where they can be left to naturalize, in the light shade beneath a tree or in a woodland garden. In mixed beds and borders, the faded leaves are hidden by the summer foliage of other plants.

Recommended

Many species, hybrids and cultivars of daffodils are available. Flowers range from 1½–6" across and can be solitary or borne in clusters. There are about 12 flower-form categories.

The cup in the center of a daffodil is called the corona, and the group of petals that surrounds the corona is called the perianth.

Features: spring flowers **Flower color:** white, yellow, peach, orange, pink, bicolored **Height:** 4–24" **Spread:** 4–12" **Hardiness:** zones 3–9

Dahlia

Dahlia

Dahlias in mixed cutting bed (above)

The variation in size, shape and color of dahlia flowers is astonishing. You are sure to find at least one that appeals to you.

Growing

Dahlias prefer **full sun**. The soil should be **fertile,** rich in **organic matter, moist** and **well drained**. All dahlias are tender, tuberous perennials treated as annuals. Tubers can be purchased and started early indoors. The tubers can also be lifted in fall and stored over the winter in slightly moist peat moss. Pot them and keep them in a bright room when they start sprouting in mid- to late winter. Deadhead to keep the plants tidy and blooming.

Tips

Dahlias make attractive, colorful additions to a mixed border. The smaller varieties make good edging plants and the larger ones make good alternatives to shrubs. Varieties with unusual or interesting flowers are attractive specimen plants.

Recommended

Of the many dahlia hybrids available, most are grown from tubers but a few can be started from seed. Many hybrids are sold based on flower shape, such as collarette, decorative or peony-flowered. The flowers range in size from 2–12" and are available in many colors. Check with your local garden center to see what is available.

Dahlia cultivars are available in a vast array of colors, sizes and flower forms but breeders have yet to develop true-blue, scented or frost-hardy selections.

Features: summer flowers; attractive foliage; bushy habit **Flower color:** purple, pink, white, yellow, orange, red, bicolored **Height:** 8–60" **Spread:** 8–18" **Hardiness:** tender perennial; grown as an annual

Flowering Onion

Allium

*F*lowering onions, with their striking, ball-like to loose, nodding clusters of flowers, are sure to attract attention in the garden.

Growing

Flowering onions grow best in **full sun**. The soil should be **average to fertile, moist** and **well drained**. Plant bulbs in fall, 2–4" deep, depending on the size of the bulb.

Tips

Flowering onions are best planted in groups in a bed or border where they can be left to naturalize. Most will self-seed when left to their own devices. The foliage, which tends to fade just as the plants come into flower, can be hidden with groundcover or a low, bushy companion plant.

A. giganteum (above), A. cernuum (below)

Recommended

Several flowering onion species, hybrids and cultivars have gained popularity for their decorative, colorful flowers. These include *A. **aflatunense***, with dense, globe-like clusters of lavender flowers; *A. **caeruleum*** (blue globe onion), with globe-like clusters of blue flowers; *A. **cernuum*** (nodding or wild onion), with loose, drooping clusters of pink flowers; and *A. **giganteum*** (giant onion), a big plant that grows up to 6' tall, with large, globe-shaped clusters of pinky purple flowers.

Although the leaves have an onion scent when bruised, the flowers are often sweetly fragrant.

Features: summer flowers; cylindrical or strap-shaped leaves **Flower color:** lavender, blue, pink, purple, yellow, maroon, pinky purple **Height:** 12–80" **Spread:** 2–12" **Hardiness:** zones 3–9

Gladiolus

Gladiolus

'Homecoming' (below)

Plant corms in spring, 4–6" deep, once the soil has warmed. Corms can also be started early indoors. Plant a few corms each week for about a month to prolong the blooming period.

Tips

Planted in groups in beds and borders, gladiolus makes a bold statement. Corms can also be pulled up in fall and stored in damp peat moss in a cool, frost-free location for the winter.

Recommended

G. x *hortulanus* is a huge group of hybrids. Gladiolus flowers come in almost every imaginable shade, except blue. Plants are commonly grouped in three classifications: **Grandiflorus** is the best known, each corm producing a single spike of large, often ruffled flowers; **Nanus**, the hardiest group, can survive in zone 3 with protection and produces several spikes of up to seven flowers; and **Primulinus** produces a single spike of up to 23 flowers that are more spaced out on the spike than those of Grandiflorus.

Perhaps best known as a cut flower, gladiolus adds an air of extravagance to the garden.

Growing

Gladiolus grows best in **full sun** but tolerates partial shade. The soil should be **fertile, humus rich, moist** and **well drained**. Flower spikes may need staking and shelter from the wind to prevent them from blowing over.

Over 10,000 cultivars of gladiolus have been developed.

Features: brightly colored, mid- to late-summer flowers **Flower color:** every shade except blue **Height:** 18–72" **Spread:** 6–12" **Hardiness:** zones 8–10; grown as an annual (some perennials to zone 3)

Lily
Lilium

*D*ecorative clusters of large, richly colored blooms grace these tall plants. Flowers are produced at different times of the season, depending on the hybrid, and it is possible to have lilies blooming all season if a variety of cultivars are chosen.

Growing

Lilies grow best in **full sun** but like to have their **roots shaded**. The soil should be rich in **organic matter, fertile, moist** and **well drained**.

Tips

Lilies are often grouped in beds and borders and can be naturalized in woodland gardens and near water features. These plants are narrow but tall; plant at least three plants together to create some volume.

Recommended

The many species, hybrids and cultivars available are grouped by type. Visit your local garden center to see what is available. The following are two popular groups of lilies. **Asiatic hybrids** bear clusters of flowers in early summer or mid-summer and are available in a wide range of colors. **Oriental hybrids** bear clusters of large, fragrant, white, pink or red flowers in mid- and late summer.

Lilies in a colorful border (above), 'Stargazer' (below)

Lily bulbs should be planted in fall before the first frost but can also be planted in spring if bulbs are available.

Features: early-, mid- or late-season flowers **Flower color:** shades of orange, yellow, peach, pink, purple, red, white **Height:** 24–60" **Spread:** 12" **Hardiness:** zones 4–8

Tulip
Tulipa

Tulips, with their beautiful, often garishly colored flowers, are a welcome sight in the warm days of spring.

Growing

Tulips grow best in **full sun**. The flowers tend to bend toward the light in light or partial shade. The soil should be **fertile** and **well drained**. Plant bulbs in fall, 4–6" deep, depending on the size of the bulb. Bulbs that have been cold treated can be planted in spring. Although tulips can repeat bloom, many hybrids perform best if planted new each year. The species and older cultivars are the best choices for naturalizing.

Tips

Tulips provide the best display when mass planted or planted in groups in flowerbeds and borders. They can also be grown in containers and can be forced to bloom early in pots indoors. Some of the species and older cultivars can be naturalized in meadow and wildflower gardens.

Recommended

There are about 100 species of tulips and thousands of hybrids and cultivars. They are generally divided into 15 groups based on bloom time and flower appearance. They come in dozens of shades, with many bicolored or multi-colored varieties. Blue is the only shade not available. Darwin Hybrids are the strongest growing tulips and are most likely to come back year after year in your garden.

During the 'tulipomania' of the 1630s the bulbs were worth many times their weight in gold, and many tulip speculators lost massive fortunes when the mania ended.

Features: spring flowers **Flower color:** all shades except blue **Height:** 6–30" **Spread:** 2–8" **Hardiness:** zones 3–8; often treated as an annual

Basil

Ocimum

The sweet, fragrant leaves of fresh basil add a delicious, licorice-like flavor to salads and tomato-based dishes.

Growing

Basil grows best in a **warm, sheltered** location in **full sun**. The soil should be **fertile, moist** and **well drained**. Pinch the tips regularly to encourage bushy growth. Plant out or direct sow seed after frost danger has passed in spring.

Tips

Although basil will grow best in a warm spot outdoors in the garden, it can be grown successfully indoors in a pot by a bright window to provide you with fresh leaves all year.

Recommended

O. basilicum is one of the most popular of the culinary herbs. There are dozens of varieties, including ones with large or tiny, green or purple and smooth or ruffled leaves.

O. basilicum 'Genovese' (above & below)

Basil is a good companion plant for tomatoes—both like warm, moist growing conditions and when you pick tomatoes for a salad you'll also remember to include a few sprigs or leaves of basil.

Features: fragrant, decorative leaves
Height: 12–24" **Spread:** 12–18"
Hardiness: tender annual

Chives

Allium

A. schoenoprasum (above & below)

The delicate onion flavor of chives is best enjoyed fresh. Mix chives into dips or sprinkle them on salads and baked potatoes.

Growing

Chives grow best in **full sun**. The soil should be **fertile, moist** and **well drained**, but chives adapt to most soil conditions. These plants are easy to start from seed, but they do like the soil temperature to stay above 65° F before they will germinate, so seeds started directly in the garden are unlikely to sprout before early summer.

Chives will spread with reckless abandon as the clumps grow larger and the plants self-seed.

Tips

Chives are decorative enough to be included in a mixed or herbaceous border and can be left to naturalize. In an herb garden, chives should be given plenty of space to allow self-seeding.

Recommended

A. schoenoprasum forms a clump of bright green, cylindrical leaves. Clusters of pinky purple flowers are produced in early and mid-summer. Varieties with white or pink flowers are available.

Chives are said to increase appetite and encourage good digestion.

Features: foliage; form; flowers **Flower color:** white, pink, pinky purple **Height:** 8–24" **Spread:** 12" or more **Hardiness:** zones 3–9

Coriander / Cilantro

Coriandrum

Coriander is a multi-purpose herb—its leaves and seeds have distinct flavors and culinary uses. The leaves are called cilantro and are used in salads, salsas and soups; the seeds are called coriander and are used in pies, chutneys and marmalades.

Growing

Coriander prefers **full sun** but tolerates partial shade. The soil should be **fertile, light** and **well drained**. These plants dislike humid conditions and do best during a dry summer.

Tips

Coriander has pungent leaves and is best planted where people will not have to brush past it. It is, however, a delight to behold when in flower. Add a plant or two here and there throughout your borders and vegetable garden, both for the visual appeal and to attract beneficial insects. Coriander dies soon after it goes to seed, so sow several crops throughout spring to ensure you have leaves to harvest all summer long.

Recommended

C. sativum forms a clump of lacy basal foliage above which large, loose clusters of tiny, white flowers are produced. The seeds ripen in late summer and fall.

C. sativum (above & below)

The delicate, cloud-like clusters of flowers attract pollinating insects, such as butterflies and bees, as well as abundant predatory insects that will help keep pest insects at a minimum in your garden.

Features: form; foliage; flowers; seeds
Flower color: white **Height:** 18–24"
Spread: 8–18" **Hardiness:** tender annual

Dill

Anethum

A. graveolens (above & below)

Growing

Dill grows best in **full sun** in a **sheltered** location out of strong winds. The soil should be of **poor to average fertility, moist** and **well drained**. Sow seeds every couple of weeks in spring and early summer to ensure a regular supply of leaves. Dill should not be grown near fennel because they will cross-pollinate and the seeds of both plants will lose their distinct flavors.

Tips

With its feathery leaves, dill is an attractive addition to a mixed bed or border. It can be included in a vegetable garden but does well in any sunny location. It also attracts predatory insects to the garden.

Recommended

A. graveolens forms a clump of feathery foliage. Clusters of yellow flowers are borne at the tops of sturdy stems.

Dill leaves and seeds are probably best known for their use as pickling herbs, though they have a wide variety of other culinary uses.

Dill turns up frequently in historical records as both a culinary and medicinal herb. It was used by the Egyptians and Romans and is mentioned in the Bible.

A popular Scandinavian dish called gravlax is made by marinating a fillet of salmon with the leaves and seeds of dill.

Features: feathery, edible foliage; summer flowers; edible seeds **Flower color:** yellow; **Height:** 24–60" **Spread:** 12" or more **Hardiness:** annual

Mint
Mentha

The cool, refreshing flavor of mint lends itself to tea and other hot or cold beverages. Mint sauce, made from freshly chopped mint leaves, is often served with lamb.

Growing
Mint grows well in **full sun** or **partial shade**. The soil should be **average to fertile, humus rich** and **moist**. These plants spread vigorously by rhizomes and may need a barrier in the soil to restrict their spread.

Tips
Mint is a good groundcover for damp spots. It grows well along ditches that may only be periodically wet. It also can be used in beds and borders, but place mint carefully because it may overwhelm less vigorous plants.

The flowers attract bees, butterflies and other pollinators to the garden.

Recommended
There are many species, hybrids and cultivars of mint. Spearmint (*M. spicata*), peppermint (*M. x piperita*) and orange mint (*M. x piperita citrata*) are three of the most commonly grown culinary varieties. There are also more decorative varieties with variegated or curly leaves as well as varieties with unusual, fruit-scented leaves.

M. x piperata 'Chocolate' (above),
M. x gracilis 'Variegata' (below)

A few sprigs of fresh mint added to a pitcher of iced tea give it an added zip.

Features: fragrant foliage; summer flowers **Flower color:** purple, pink, white **Height:** 6–36" **Spread:** 36" or more **Hardiness:** zones 4–8

Oregano / Marjoram
Origanum

O. vulgare 'Aureum' (above & below)

Growing
Oregano and marjoram grow best in **full sun**. The soil should be of **poor to average fertility, neutral to alkaline** and **well drained**. The flowers attract pollinators to the garden.

Tips
These bushy perennials make a lovely addition to any border and can be trimmed to form low hedges.

Recommended
O. majorana (marjoram) is upright and shrubby with light green, hairy leaves. It bears white or pink flowers in summer and can be grown as an annual where it is not hardy.

O. vulgare var. *hirtum* (oregano, Greek oregano) is the most flavorful culinary variety of oregano. The low, bushy plant has hairy, gray-green leaves and bears white flowers. Many other interesting varieties of *O. vulgare* are available, including those with golden, variegated or curly leaves.

Oregano and marjoram are two of the best known and most frequently used herbs. They are popular in stuffings, soups and stews, and no pizza is complete until it has been sprinkled with fresh or dried oregano leaves.

In Greek oros means 'mountain' and ganos means 'joy and beauty,' so oregano translates as 'joy or beauty of the mountain.'

Features: fragrant foliage; summer flowers; bushy habit **Flower color:** white, pink **Height:** 12–32" **Spread:** 8–18" **Hardiness:** zones 5–9

Parsley
Petroselinium

P. crispum (above & below)

Although parsley is usually used as a garnish, it is rich in vitamins and minerals and is reputed to freshen the breath after garlic- or onion-rich foods are eaten.

Growing
Parsley grows well in **full sun** or **partial shade**. The soil should be of **average to rich fertility, humus rich, moist** and **well drained**. Direct sow seeds because the plants resent transplanting. If you start seeds early, use peat pots so the plants can be potted or planted out without disruption.

Tips
Parsley should be started where you mean to grow it as it doesn't transplant well. Containers of parsley can be kept close to the house for easy picking. The bright green leaves and compact growth habit make parsley a good edging plant for beds and borders.

Recommended
P. crispum forms a clump of bright green, divided leaves. This plant is a biennial but is usually grown as an annual because the leaves are the desired parts, not the flowers or the seeds. Cultivars may have flat or curly leaves. Flat leaves are more flavorful and curly are more decorative. Dwarf cultivars are also available.

Parsley leaves make a tasty and nutritious addition to salads. Tear freshly picked leaves and sprinkle them over or mix them in your mixed greens.

Features: attractive foliage **Height:** 8–24" **Spread:** 12–24" **Hardiness:** zones 5–8; grown as an annual

Rosemary

Rosmarinus

R. officinalis (above & below)

well drained and of **poor to average fertility**. These tender shrubs must be moved indoors for the winter.

Tips

Rosemary is often grown in a shrub border where hardy. In Michigan, where rosemary is not hardy, it is usually grown in a container as a specimen or with other plants. Low-growing, spreading plants can be included in a rock garden or along the top of a retaining wall or can be grown in hanging baskets.

Recommended

R. officinalis is a dense, bushy evergreen shrub with narrow, dark green leaves. The habit varies somewhat between cultivars from strongly upright to prostrate and spreading. Flowers are usually in shades of blue, but pink-flowered cultivars are available. Cultivars are available that can survive in zone 6 in a sheltered location with winter protection. The plants rarely reach their mature size when grown in containers.

The needle-like leaves of rosemary are used to flavor a wide variety of culinary dishes, including chicken, pork, lamb, rice, tomato and egg dishes.

Growing

Rosemary prefers **full sun** but tolerates partial shade. The soil should be

To overwinter a container-grown plant, keep it in very light or partial shade outdoors in summer, then put it in a sunny window indoors for winter and keep it well watered but allow it to dry out slightly between waterings.

Features: fragrant, evergreen foliage; summer flowers **Flower color:** bright blue, sometimes pink **Height:** 8–48" **Spread:** 12–48" **Hardiness:** zones 8–10

Sage
Salvia

Sage is perhaps best known as a flavoring for stuffing, but it has a great range of uses, and is often included in soups, stews, sausages and dumplings.

Growing

Sage prefers **full sun** but tolerates light shade. The soil should be of **average fertility** and **well drained**. These plants benefit from a light mulch of compost each year. They are drought tolerant once established.

Tips

Sage is an attractive plant for the border, adding volume to the middle of the border or as an attractive edging or feature plant near the front. Sage can also be grown in mixed planters.

Recommended

S. officinalis is a woody, mounding plant with soft, gray-green leaves. Spikes of light purple flowers appear in early and midsummer. Many cultivars with attractive foliage are available, including the silver-leaved **'Berggarten,'** the purple-leaved **'Icterina,'** the yellow-margined **'Purpurea,'** and the purple, green and cream variegated **'Tricolor,'** which has a pink flush to the new growth.

S. officinalis 'Icterina' (above), 'Purpurea' (below)

Sage has been used since at least ancient Greek times as a medicinal and culinary herb and continues to be widely used for both those purposes today.

Features: fragrant, decorative foliage; summer flowers **Flower color:** blue, purple **Height:** 12–24" **Spread:** 18–36" **Hardiness:** zones 5–8

Tarragon
Artemisia

A. dracunculus var. *sativa* (above)

There are two types of tarragon available. French tarragon is the preferred culinary selection, while Russian tarragon is a weedy plant that is grown from seed but has little of the desired flavor. French tarragon is grown from cuttings. Chew a leaf from the plant and if you don't notice the distinctive licorice flavor don't buy it.

The distinctive licorice flavor of tarragon lends itself to a wide variety of meat and vegetable dishes and is the key flavoring in Bernaise sauce.

Growing
Tarragon grows best in **full sun.** The soil should be **average to fertile, moist** and **well drained.** Divide the plants every few years to keep them growing vigorously and to encourage the best flavored leaves.

Tips
These plants are not exceptionally decorative and can be included in an herb garden or mixed border where their tall stems will be supported by the surrounding plants.

Recommended
A. dracunculus* var. *sativa (French or German Tarragon) is a bushy plant with tall stems and narrow leaves. Airy clusters of insignificant flowers are produced in late summer.

Features: foliage **Height:** 18–36"
Spread: 12–18" **Hardiness:** zones 3–8

Thyme
Thymus

Thyme is a popular culinary herb used when cooking soups, stews, casseroles and roasts.

Growing
Thyme prefers **full sun**. The soil should be **neutral to alkaline** and of **poor to average fertility**. **Good drainage** is essential. It is beneficial to work leaf mold and sharp limestone gravel into the soil to improve structure and drainage.

Tips
Thyme is useful for sunny, dry locations at the front of borders, between or beside paving stones, on rock gardens and rock walls and in containers.

Once the plants have finished flowering, shear them back by about half to encourage new growth and to prevent the plants from becoming too woody.

Recommended
T. x citriodorus (lemon-scented thyme) forms a mound of lemon-scented, dark green foliage. The flowers are pale pink. Cultivars with silver- or gold-margined leaves are available.

T. vulgaris (common thyme) forms a bushy mound of dark green leaves. The flowers may be purple, pink or white. Cultivars with variegated leaves are available.

T. vulgaris (above), *T.* x *citriodorus* (below)

These plants are bee magnets when blooming; thyme honey is pleasantly herbal and goes very well with biscuits.

Features: bushy habit; fragrant, decorative foliage; flowers **Flower color:** purple, pink, white **Height:** 8–16" **Spread:** 8–16" **Hardiness:** zones 4–9

Fescue

Festuca

F. glauca 'Elijah Blue' (above), *F. glauca* (below)

This fine-leaved ornamental grass forms tufted clumps that resemble pincushions. Its metallic blue coloring is an all-season cooling accent for the garden.

Growing

Fescue thrives in **full sun to light shade**. The soil should be of **average fertility, moist** and **well drained**. Plants are drought tolerant once established. Fescue emerges early in spring, so shear it back to 1" above the crown in late winter, before new growth emerges. Shear off flower stalks just above the foliage to keep the plant tidy or to prevent self-seeding.

Tips

With its fine texture and distinct blue color, this grass can be used as a single specimen in a rock garden or a container planting. Plant fescue in drifts or to edge a bed, border or pathway. It looks attractive in both formal and informal gardens.

Recommended

F. glauca (blue fescue) forms tidy, tufted clumps of fine, blue-toned foliage and panicles of flowers in May and June. Cultivars and hybrids come in varying heights and in shades ranging from blue to olive green. **'Elijah Blue,' 'Boulder Blue,' 'Skinner's Blue'** and **'Solling'** are popular selections.

Also called: blue fescue **Features:** blue to blue-green foliage; color that persists into winter; habit **Height:** 6–12" **Spread:** 10–12" **Hardiness:** zones 3–8

Flowering Fern

Osmunda

$\mathcal{F}$erns have a certain pre-historic mystique and can add a graceful elegance and textural accent to the garden.

Growing

Flowering ferns prefer **light shade** but tolerate full sun if the soil is consistently moist. The soil should be **fertile, humus rich, acidic** and **moist**. Flowering ferns tolerate wet soil and will spread as offsets form at the plant bases.

Tips

These large ferns form an attractive mass when planted in large colonies. They can be included in beds and borders and make a welcome addition to a woodland garden.

Recommended

O. cinnamomea (cinnamon fern) has light green fronds that fan out in a circular fashion from a central point. Bright green, leafless, fertile fronds that mature to cinnamon brown are produced in spring and stand straight up in the center of the plant.

O. regalis (royal fern) forms a dense clump of foliage. Feathery, flower-like, fertile fronds stand out among the sterile fronds in summer and mature to a rusty brown. **'Purpurescens'** fronds are purple-red

O. regalis (above & below)

when they emerge in spring and then mature to green. This contrasts well with the purple stems. (Zones 3–8)

The flowering fern's 'flowers' are actually its spore-producing sporangia.

Features: deciduous, perennial fern; decorative, fertile fronds; habit **Height:** 30"–5' **Spread:** 2–3' **Hardiness:** zones 2–8

Fountain Grass

Pennisetum

P. setaceum 'Purpureum' (above & below)

Fountain grass's low maintenance and graceful form make it easy to place. It will soften any landscape, even in winter.

Growing

Fountain grass thrives in **full sun**. The soil should be of **average fertility** and **well drained**. Plants are drought tolerant once established. Plants may self-seed, but are not troublesome. Shear perennials back in early spring and divide them when they start to die out in the center.

Tips

Fountain grasses can be used as individual specimen plants, in group plantings and drifts, or combined with flowering annuals, perennials, shrubs and other ornamental grasses. Annual selections are often planted in containers or beds for height and stature.

Recommended

Both perennial and annual fountain grasses exist. Popular perennials include *P. alopecuroides* 'Hameln' (dwarf perennial fountain grass), a compact cultivar with silvery white plumes and narrow, dark green foliage that turns gold in fall (zones 5–8) and *P. orientale* (Oriental fountain grass), with tall, blue-green foliage and large, silvery white flowers (zones 6–8, with winter protection). Annual fountain grasses include *P. setaceum* (annual fountain grass), which has narrow, green foliage and pinkish purple flowers that mature to gray. Its cultivar **'Rubrum'** (red annual fountain grass) has broader, deep burgundy foliage and pinkish purple flowers. *P. glaucum* **'Purple Majesty'** (purple ornamental millet) has blackish purple foliage and coarse, bottlebrush flowers. Its form resembles a corn stalk.

The name Pennisetum alopecuroides *refers to the plumy flower spikes that resemble a fox's tail. In Latin,* penna *means 'feather' and* seta *means 'bristle';* alopekos *is the Greek word for fox.*

Features: arching, fountain-like habit; silvery pink to purplish black foliage; flowers; winter interest **Flower color:** silvery white, pinkish purple **Height:** 2–5' **Spread:** 2–3' **Hardiness:** zones 5–9 or annual

Hakone Grass

Hakonechloa

Hakone grass is an attractive, shade-loving grass that provides interest throughout the growing season.

Growing

Hakone grass prefers **light shade** or **partial shade** but tolerates full sun if the soil is kept moist. The soil should be **fertile, rich in organic matter, moist** and **well drained**. Use an organic mulch to maintain soil moisture as these plants resent drying out. If the foliage becomes scorched, move the plant to a more shaded location. Mulch well in winter to protect the plants.

Tips

Hakone grass is one of the few grass plants that grows well in shaded locations. Its texture and color is a good contrast to broad-leaved shade plants. This grass makes an attractive addition to mixed beds and borders and can be used along the tops of retaining walls where its arching habit will show well.

Recommended

H. macra has bright green, arching, grass-like foliage. The foliage turns deep pink in fall, then bronze as winter sets in. Several cultivars are available. **'Albo-Striata'** has leaves that are green and white striped. **'All Gold'** has pure gold leaves and is more upright

H. macra 'Aureola' (above & below)

and spiky in habit. **'Aureola'** has bright yellow foliage with narrow, green streaks; the foliage turns pink in fall. Yellow-leaved cultivars may scorch in full sun and lose their yellow color in too much shade.

Hakone grass is native to Japan, where it grows on mountainsides and cliffsides, often near streams and other water sources.

Features: arching habit; fall color
Height: 12–24" **Spread:** 12–24"
Hardiness: zones 5–9

Maidenhair Fern

Adiantum

A. pedatum (above & below)

These charming and delicate-looking native ferns add a graceful touch to any woodland planting. Their unique habit and texture will stand out in any garden.

Growing

Maidenhair fern grows well in **light to partial shade** but tolerates full shade. The soil should be of **average fertility, humus rich, slightly acidic** and **moist**. This plant rarely needs dividing, but it can be divided in spring to propagate more plants.

Tips

These lovely ferns will do well in any shaded spot in the garden. Include them in rock gardens, woodland gardens, shaded borders and beneath shade trees. They also make an attractive addition to a shaded planting next to a water feature or on a slope where the foliage can be seen when it sways in the breeze.

Recommended

A. pedatum forms a spreading mound of delicate, arching fronds. Its light green leaflets stand out against the black stems, and the whole plant turns bright yellow in fall. Spores are produced on the undersides of the leaflets.

Try growing the fine-textured and delicate maidenhair fern with Hostas, Pulmonarias *or* Brunneras. *It will create a nice contrast in texture.*

Also called: northern maidenhair
Features: deciduous, perennial fern; summer and fall foliage; habit **Height:** 12–24"
Spread: 12–24" **Hardiness:** zones 2–8

Male Fern

Dryopteris

D. *filix-mas* (above)

This is a lovely, easy-to-grow fern with several interesting cultivars that provide unusual, crinkled or crested fronds.

Growing

Male fern grows best in **partial shade** but tolerates full sun in wet soil. The soil should be **fertile, humus rich** and **moist**. Divide the plant to control spread and to propagate.

Tips

Male ferns are large, impressive ferns that are useful in a shaded area or a woodland garden. This is an ideal fern to include in an area of the garden that stays moist or periodically floods.

Recommended

D. filix-mas forms a clump of lacy fronds. Many cultivars with decorative and sometimes unusual frond variations are available. Some of the most popular include '**Cristata,**' with crested frond tips; '**Linearis,**' with very narrow frond leaflets and '**Nana,**' a dwarf form that grows about 6" tall.

This is one of the easiest ferns to grow and one of the hardiest.

Features: decorative fronds; varied cultivars
Height: 30–48" **Spread:** 24–36" **Hardiness:** zones 3–8

Miscanthus

Miscanthus

M. sinensis var. purpurescens (above)

Miscanthus is one of the most popular and majestic of all the ornamental grasses. Its graceful foliage dances in the wind and makes an impressive sight all year long.

Growing

Miscanthus prefers **full sun**. The soil should be of **average fertility, moist** and **well drained,** though some selections tolerate wet soil. All selections are drought tolerant once established.

Tips

Give these magnificent beauties room to grow so you can fully appreciate their form. The plant's height will determine the best place for each selection in the border. Miscanthus creates dramatic impact in groups or as seasonal screens.

Recommended

There are many available cultivars of **M. sinensis**, all distinguished by the white midrib on the leaf blade. Some popular selections include **'Gracillimus'** (maiden grass), with long, fine-textured leaves; **'Grosse Fontaine'** (large fountain), a tall, wide-spreading, early-flowering selection; **'Morning Light'** (variegated maiden grass), a short and delicate plant with fine, white leaf edges; **var. *purpurescens*** (flame grass), with foliage that turns bright orange in early fall; and **'Strictus'** (porcupine grass), a tall, stiff, upright selection with unusual, horizontal, yellow bands.

The flowerheads make an interesting addition to fresh or dried flower arrangements.

Also called: eulalia, Japanese silver grass **Features:** upright, arching habit; colorful summer and fall foliage; late-summer and fall flowers; winter interest **Flower color:** pink, copper, silver **Height:** 4–8' **Spread:** 2–4' **Hardiness:** zones 5–9, possibly zone 4

New York Fern

Thelypteris

This fern is native to most of the East Coast and is found as far north as Newfoundland and as far south as Georgia.

Growing

New York ferns grow well in **full sun, light shade** or **partial shade**. The soil should be of **average fertility, humus rich, slightly acidic** and **consistently moist**. Divide the plants regularly or pull up extra plants to control the vigorous spread.

This lovely fern is quick spreading and is useful for filling lightly shaded locations.

Tips

New York fern makes an attractive addition to a shaded garden and can be used in a moist border or near a water feature if your garden includes one. This native fern is best used in gardens where there is plenty of room for it to spread.

Recommended

T. noveboracensis is an upright fern with gently arching, yellow-green fronds. Plants spread quickly by rhizomes.

Features: foliage; tolerates moist soil **Height:** 18"
Spread: 16–40" **Hardiness:** zones 3–8

Ostrich Fern

Matteuccia

M. struthiopteris (above & below)

These popular, classic ferns are revered for their delicious, emerging spring fronds and their stately vase-shaped habit.

Growing

Ostrich fern prefers **partial or light shade** but tolerates full shade or even full sun if the soil is kept moist. The soil should be **average to fertile, humus rich, neutral to acidic** and **moist**. The leaves may scorch if the soil is not moist enough. These ferns are aggressive spreaders that reproduce by spores. Unwanted plants can be pulled up and composted or given away.

Tips

Ostrich fern appreciates a moist woodland garden and is often found growing wild alongside woodland streams and creeks. Useful in shaded borders, these plants are quick to spread, to the delight of those who enjoy the young fronds as a culinary delicacy.

Recommended

M. struthiopteris (*M. pennsylvanica*) forms a circular cluster of slightly arching, feathery fronds. Stiff, brown, fertile fronds, covered in reproductive spores, stick up in the center of the cluster in late summer and persist through winter. These ferns are a popular addition to dried arrangements.

Ostrich ferns are also grown commercially for their edible fiddleheads. The tightly coiled, new spring fronds taste delicious lightly steamed and served with butter. Remove the bitter, reddish brown, papery coating before steaming.

Also called: fiddlehead fern **Features:** perennial fern; foliage; habit **Height:** 3–5' **Spread:** 1–3' or more **Hardiness:** zones 1–8

Painted Fern / Lady Fern

Athyrium

A. niponicum var. *pictum* (above & below)

Lady ferns and painted ferns are some of the most well-behaved ferns, adding color and texture to shady spots without growing out of control.

Growing

Lady and painted ferns grow well in **full shade, partial shade** or **light shade**. The soil should be of **average fertility, humus rich, acidic** and **moist**. Division is rarely required but can be done to propagate more plants.

Tips

Lady and painted ferns form an attractive mass of foliage, but they don't grown out of control like some ferns tend to. Include them in shade gardens and moist woodland gardens.

Recommended

A. filix-femina (lady fern) forms a dense clump of lacy fronds. It grows 12–24" tall and has a 24" spread. Cultivars are available, including dwarf cultivars and cultivars with variable foliage.

A. niponicum var. *pictum* '**Metallicum**' (Japanese painted fern) forms a clump of dark green fronds with a silvery or reddish metallic sheen. It grows 12–24" tall and has a 24" spread. Many cultivars of *A. niponicum* var. *pictum* are available. Some of the more colorful cultivars include '**Burgundy Lace,**' with metallic burgundy leaves; '**Pewter Lace,**' with fine, metallic gray foliage and '**Ursula's Red,**' with iridescent, silver white and rich, maroon red leaves. (Zones 4–8)

Features: habit; foliage **Height:** 12–24"
Spread: 12–24" **Hardiness:** zones 3–8

Reed Grass
Calamagrostis

C. x acutiflora 'Karl Foerster' (above & below)

This is a graceful, metamorphic grass that changes its habit and flower color throughout the seasons. The slightest breeze keeps this grass in perpetual motion.

Growing

Reed grass grows best in **full sun**. The soil should be **fertile, moist** and **well drained**. Heavy clay and dry soils are tolerated. It may be susceptible to rust in cool, wet summers or in sites with poor air circulation. Rain and heavy snow may cause reed grass to flop temporarily, but it quickly bounces back. Cut back the plant to 2–4" in very early spring before growth begins. Divide reed grass if it begins to die out in the center.

Tips

Whether used as a single, stately focal point in small groupings or in large drifts, reed grass is a desirable, low-maintenance grass. It combines well with late-summer and fall-blooming perennials.

Recommended

C. x *acutiflora* '**Karl Foerster'** (Foerster's feather reed grass), the most popular selection, forms a loose mound of green foliage from which the airy, distinctly vertical, bottlebrush flowers emerge in June. The flowering stems have a loose, arching habit when they first emerge but grow more stiff and upright over summer. Other cultivars include '**Overdam,'** a compact, less hardy selection with white leaf edges. Watch for a new introduction called '**Avalanche,'** which has a white center stripe.

If you like the way reed grass holds its flowers high above its mounded foliage, you might also like Deschampsia *(tufted hair grass) and* Molinia *(moor grass) and their species and cultivars. Some have creamy yellow, striped foliage.*

Features: open habit; green foliage turns bright gold in fall; winter interest **Flower color:** silvery pink, tan **Height:** 3–5' **Spread:** 2–3' **Hardiness:** zones 4–9

Sweet Flag

Acorus

These grass-like plants are most at home in wet and boggy locations, making them a favorite of water gardeners.

Growing

Sweet flags grow best in **full sun**. The soil should be **fertile** and **moist or wet**. Divide plants to propagate and to prevent clumps from becoming too dense.

Tips

These plants are much admired for their habit as well as for the wonderful, spicy fragrance of the crushed leaves. Include sweet flag in moist borders or at the margins of your pond if you have one. They can also be grown in containers.

Recommended

A. calamus (sweet flag) is a large, clump-forming plant with long, narrow, bright green, fragrant foliage. It grows 24–60" tall with about a 24" spread. **'Variegatus'** is a popular and commonly available cultivar that has yellow, cream and green vertically striped leaves.

A. gramineus (Japanese rush, dwarf sweet flag) is a smaller, clump-forming plant with glossy, green, fragrant leaves. It grows 4–12" tall with an equal spread. The cultivar **'Ogon'** is prized for its bright, golden, variegated foliage. (Zones 5–8)

A. gramineus 'Variegatus' (above & below)

Sweet flag was a popular moat-side plant in the past, and the fragrant leaves were spread on floors to keep rooms smelling sweet.

Features: attractive habit and foliage **Height:** 4–60"
Spread: 4–24" **Hardiness:** zones 4–8

Switch Grass

Panicum

P. virgatum 'Heavy Metal' (above & below)

Growing

Switch grass thrives in **full sun, light shade** or **partial shade**. The soil should be of **average fertility** and **well drained**, though the plants adapt to both moist and dry soils and tolerate conditions ranging from heavy clay to lighter, sandy soil. Cut switch grass back to 2–4" from the ground in early spring. The flower stems may break under heavy, wet snow or in exposed, windy sites.

Tips

Plant switch grass singly in small gardens, in large groups in spacious borders, or at the edges of ponds or pools for a dramatic, whimsical effect. The seedheads attract birds and the foliage changes color in fall, so place this plant where you can enjoy both of these features.

Recommended

P. virgatum (switch grass) is suited to wild meadow gardens. Some of its popular cultivars include **'Heavy Metal'** (blue switch grass), an upright plant with narrow, steely blue foliage flushed with gold and burgundy in fall; **'Prairie Sky'** (blue switch grass), an arching plant with deep blue foliage; and **'Shenandoah'** (red switch grass), with red-tinged green foliage that turns burgundy in fall.

A native to the prairie grasslands, switch grass naturalizes equally well in an informal border or a natural meadow.

Switch grass's delicate, airy panicles fill gaps in the garden border and can be cut for fresh or dried arrangements.

Features: clumping habit; green, blue or burgundy foliage; airy panicles of flowers; fall color; winter interest **Height:** 3–5' **Spread:** 30–36" **Hardiness:** zones 3–9

Glossary

Acid soil: soil with a pH lower than 7.0

Alkaline soil: soil with a pH higher than 7.0

Annual: a plant that germinates, flowers, sets seed and dies in one growing season

Aril: a fleshy outer covering or outgrowth of some seeds

Basal leaves: leaves that form from the crown, at the base of the plant

Bract: a modified leaf at the base of a flower or flower cluster

Companion plant: a plant positioned close to another because of its beneficial effects, such as the ability to discourage pests and improve growth

Corm: a bulb-like, food-storing, underground stem that resembles a bulb without scales

Cultivar: a cultivated plant variety with one or more distinct differences from the species, e.g. in flower color or disease resistance

Deadhead: to remove spent flowers to maintain a neat appearance and encourage a longer blooming season

Direct sow: to sow seeds directly into the garden

Dormancy: a period of plant inactivity, usually during winter or unfavorable conditions

Espalier: A tree trained from a young age to grow on a single plane—often along a wall or a fence

Genus: a category of biological classification between the species and family levels; the first word in a scientific name indicates the genus

Hardy: capable of surviving seemingly unfavorable conditions, such as cold weather or frost, without protection

Humus: decomposed or decomposing organic material in the soil

Hybrid: a plant resulting from natural or human-induced crossbreeding between varieties, species or genera

Inflorescence: the flowering part of a plant and the specific arrangement of the flowers on the plant

Neutral soil: soil with a pH of 7.0

Offset: a horizontal branch that forms at the base of a plant and produces new plants from buds at its tips

Panicle: a compound flower structure with groups of flowers on short stalks

Perennial: a plant that takes three or more years to complete its life cycle

pH: a measure of acidity or alkalinity; the soil pH influences availability of nutrients for plants

Picotee: a narrow band of color on the edge of a petal

Pinch: a common gardening technique that involves removing the growing tips of the plants by pinching them with your fingers. This allows side branches to develop into a bushier plant.

Rhizome: a root-like, food-storing stem that grows horizontally at or just below soil level, from which new shoots may emerge

Rootball: the root mass and surrounding soil of a plant

Seedhead: dried, inedible fruit that contains seeds; the fruiting stage of the inflorescence

Self-seeding: reproducing by means of seeds without human assistance, so that new plants constantly replace those that die

Sepals: the outermost flower structures, which usually enclose the other flower parts

Spathe: one or two bracts enclosing a flower cluster

Species: the fundamental unit of biological classification; the entity from which cultivars and varieties are derived

Specimen plant: a striking plant in prime condition, grown where it can be seen clearly

Sucker: a shoot that grows from the root, often some distance from the plant; it can be separated to form a new plant once it develops its own roots

Tender: incapable of surviving the climatic conditions of a given region and requiring protection from frost or cold

Tuber: the thick section of a rhizome bearing nodes and buds

Variegation: foliage that has more than one color, often patched or striped or bearing leaf margins of a different color

Variety: a naturally occurring variant of a species

Index of Plant Names

Entries in **bold** type indicate the main plant headings. Entries in *italics* indicate scientific names.

About the Authors

Tim Wood is a third-generation horticulturist who started his career at his family's nursery at the age of eight. He is now Product Development Manager for Spring Meadow Nursery, a national wholesale propagation nursery based in Grand Haven, Michigan. Tim holds a master's degree in Ornamental Horticulture from Michigan State University. His articles and photographs have appeared in *American Nurseryman, Garden Center Magazine, Country Living Gardener, Midwest Living* and *Better Homes and Gardens*. Tim is a nationally recognized speaker who addresses horticulture organizations across the United States.

Alison Beck has gardened since she was a child. She has a diploma in Horticulture and a degree in Creative Writing. Alison is the co-author of several best-selling gardening guides. Her books showcase her talent for practical advice and her passion for gardening.